EXAM QUESTION PRACTICE PACK

AQA GCSE (9–1)
RELIGIOUS STUDIES A

Hachette UK's policy is to use papers that are natural, renewable and recyclable products and made from wood grown in sustainable forests. The logging and manufacturing processes are expected to conform to the environmental regulations of the country of origin.

Orders: please contact Bookpoint Ltd, 130 Park Drive, Milton Park, Abingdon, Oxon OX14 4SE.
Telephone: (44) 01235 827827. Fax: (44) 01235 400401. Email education@bookpoint.co.uk Lines are open from 9 a.m. to 5 p.m., Monday to Saturday, with a 24-hour message answering service. You can also order through our website: www.hoddereducation.co.uk

ISBN: 978 1 5104 3354 0

© Hodder & Stoughton Ltd 2018

First published in 2018 by
Hodder Education,
An Hachette UK Company
Carmelite House
50 Victoria Embankment
London EC4Y 0DZ

www.hoddereducation.co.uk

Impression number   10 9 8 7 6 5 4 3

Year   2022   2021   2020   2019

Copyright notice

Cover image reproduced by permission of Fotolia/hongyphoto

Typeset by Aptara, India

Printed by Hobbs the Printers Ltd, Totton, Hampshire SO40 3WX

A catalogue record for this title is available from the British Library.

CONTENTS

INTRODUCTION

This pack of exam-style questions, example responses and mark schemes is specially curated for the AQA GCSE (9–1) Religious Studies A specification. The pack is divided into two sections:

➤ **Exam questions**. A bank of questions similar to those found in AQA GCSE (9–1) Religious Studies A papers. You may wish to photocopy all or part of them for use with your class.

➤ **Example responses and mark schemes.** For each question, there are two student responses – a 'Student A' response that is typical of an answer receiving high marks, and a 'Student B' response that would receive fewer marks. Each response includes examiner-style commentary which describes why they receive the marks they do. The mark scheme for each question indicates how the responses can be graded, and can be used alongside each type of student answer or just with the question.

The pack is designed to help you to:

➤ encourage students to reflect on their responses and ensure they know how to succeed

➤ cultivate students' key skills and knowledge by regular assessment throughout the course, or in the revision period before the exams

➤ incorporate question practice into your lesson plans in the final, vital stage of teaching a topic: putting theory into practice

➤ teach flexibly, picking and choosing photocopiable pages as appropriate to share with students

➤ facilitate peer discussion of what is good or better about given answers, which allows greater insight into quality responses

➤ allow students to analyse responses without the bias that can come from looking at their own or their friends' work and so get more from the task

Assessment objectives (AOs)

Assessment objectives are set by Ofqual and are the same across all GCSE Religious Studies A specifications and all exam boards.

The exams will measure how students have achieved the following assessment objectives.

AO1	Demonstrate knowledge and understanding of religion and beliefs, including: beliefs, practices and sources of authority influence on individuals, communities and societies similarities and differences within and/or between religions and beliefs.
AO2	Analyse and evaluate aspects of religion and belief, including their significance and influence.

Assessment objectives weightings for GCSE Religious Studies A

Assessment objectives (AOs)	Component weightings (approx. %)		Overall weighting (approx. %)
	Paper 1	Paper 2	
AO1	25	25	50
AO2	25	25	50
Overall weighting of components	50	50	100

Assessment weightings

The marks awarded on the papers will be scaled to meet the weighting of the components. Students' final marks will be calculated by adding together the scaled marks for each component. Grade boundaries will be set using this total scaled mark. The scaling and total scaled marks are shown in the table below.

Component	Maximum raw mark	Scaling factor	Maximum scaled mark
Paper 1 Section A	51	1	51
Paper 1 Section B	51	1	51
Paper 2	99	1.03	102
Total scaled marks			204

Spelling, punctuation and grammar (SPaG)

Spelling, punctuation and grammar will be assessed in some of 12-mark questions beliefs on Component 1; the best of the four answered on Component 2 against the following criteria.

Level	Performance descriptor	Marks awarded
High performance	• Learners spell and punctuate with consistent accuracy • Learners use rules of grammar with effective control of meaning overall • Learners use a wide range of specialist terms as appropriate	3
Intermediate performance	• Learners spell and punctuate with considerable accuracy • Learners use rules of grammar with general control of meaning overall • Learners use a good range of specialist terms as appropriate	2
Threshold performance	• Learners spell and punctuate with reasonable accuracy • Learners use rules of grammar with some control of meaning and any errors do not significantly hinder meaning overall • Learners use a limited range of specialist terms as appropriate	1
No marks awarded	• The learner writes nothing • The learner's response does not relate to the question • The learner's achievement in SPaG does not reach the threshold level, for example errors in spelling, punctuation and grammar severely hinder meaning	0

EXAM QUESTIONS

Paper 1 The study of religions: beliefs, teachings and practices

Christianity

1   **(a)** Which of the following is not a member of the Trinity?

    A Father ☐   **C** Son ☐

    B God ☐   **D** Holy Spirit ☐

    (1 mark)

    (b) Give **two** characteristics of God. **(2 marks)**

    (c) Explain **two** ways belief in the incarnation of Jesus influences Christians today. **(4 marks)**

    (d) Explain **two** Christian teachings about salvation. Refer to sacred writings or another source of Christian belief and teaching in your answer. **(5 marks)**

(e) 'All Christians should believe the Genesis creation story as the truth.' Evaluate this statement. In your answer you should:
  ➤ refer to Christian teaching
  ➤ give developed arguments to support this statement
  ➤ give developed arguments to support a different point of view
  ➤ reach a justified conclusion. **(12 marks)**

....

....

....

....

....

....

....

....

....

....

Total: 24 marks

(Example student responses and mark scheme on p. 33)

2 **(a)** Which of the following is a festival that remembers the resurrection of Jesus?

A	Christmas ☐	**C**	Lent ☐
B	Good Friday ☐	**D**	Easter ☐

(1 mark)

(b) Give **two** Christian forms of worship. **(2 marks)**

....

....

(c) Explain **two** contrasting ways in which prayer is carried out in Christianity. **(4 marks)**

....

....

....

....

(d) Explain **two** ways in which the Church has worked in the local community. Refer to sacred writings or another source of Christian belief and teaching in your answer **(5 marks)**

(e) 'Religious organisations should focus their work only on communities in the UK.' Evaluate this statement. In your answer you should:
- refer to Christian teaching
- give developed arguments to support this statement
- give developed arguments to support a different point of view
- reach a justified conclusion. **(12 marks)**

Total: 24 marks

(Example student responses and mark scheme on p. 38)

Islam

1   (a) Which of the following is not one of the Six Articles of Sunni Islam?

    A   Angels ☐   C   Judgement Day ☐

    B   Holy Books ☐   D   Five Pillars ☐

(1 mark)

(b) Give **two** characteristics of God in Islam.   **(2 marks)**

....

....

(c) Explain **two** ways in which belief in angels influences Muslims today.   **(4 marks)**

....

....

....

....

(d) Explain **two** Muslim teachings about Tawhid. Refer to sacred writings or another source of Muslim belief and teaching in your answer   **(5 marks)**

....

....

....

....

....

(e) 'The Qur'an is the only source of guidance needed by Muslims in their lives today.' Evaluate this statement. In your answer you should:
  - refer to Muslim teaching
  - give developed arguments to support this statement
  - give developed arguments to support a different point of view
  - reach a justified conclusion.   **(12 marks)**

....

....

....

....

....

....

....

....

....

Total: 24 marks

(Example student responses and mark scheme on p. 44)

2 **(a)** Which of the following Shi'a Obligations means 'Expressing love towards God'?

    A Nahi Anil-Munkar ☐   **C** Amr bil-Ma'oof ☐

    B Tawalla ☐   **D** Tabarra ☐

            (1 mark)

  (b) Give **two** benefits of giving Zakah.   **(2 marks)**

....

....

....

....

  (c) Explain **two** contrasting views on the origins of Ashura.   **(4 marks)**

....

....

....

....

  (d) Explain **two** ways that Salah is important to Muslims. Refer to sacred writings or another source of Muslim belief and teaching in your answer.   **(5 marks)**

....

....

....

....

....

(e) 'Hajj is the most important Pillar of Islam.' Evaluate this statement. In your answer you should:

> refer to Muslim teaching
> give developed arguments to support this statement
> give developed arguments to support a different point of view
> reach a justified conclusion.

(12 marks)

....

....

....

....

....

....

....

....

....

Total: 24 marks

(Example student responses and mark scheme on p. 48)

Paper 2A Thematic Studies
Sample set 1

Theme A: Relationships and families

1 **(a)** Which of the following is the correct term for the cancellation of a marriage?

    A divorce ☐   **C** adultery ☐

    B celibacy ☐   **D** annulment ☐

(1 mark)

  (b) Give **two** names for types of families.

(2 marks)

....

....

....

(c) Explain **two** contrasting beliefs in contemporary British society about sex before marriage. In your answer you should refer to the main religious tradition of Great Britain and one or more other religious traditions. **(4 marks)**

(d) Explain **two** teachings about marriage. Refer to sacred writings or another source of religious belief and teaching in your answer. **(5 marks)**

(e) 'For a religious couple divorce should not be allowed.' Evaluate this statement. In your answer you:
- should give reasoned arguments in support of this statement
- should give reasoned arguments to support a different point of view
- should refer to religious arguments
- may refer to non-religious arguments
- should reach a justified conclusion. **(12 marks)**

....

....

Total: 24 marks

(Example student responses and mark scheme on p. 53)

2   Explain **two** similar religious beliefs about gender equality. In your answer you must refer to one or more religious traditions.   **(4 marks)**

....

....

....

Total: 4 marks

(Example student responses and mark scheme on p. 59)

3   Explain **two** contrasting religious beliefs about divorce. In your answer you must refer to one or more religious traditions.   **(4 marks)**

....

....

....

Total: 4 marks

(Example student responses and mark scheme on p. 61)

Theme B: Religion and life

1   **(a)** Which of the following theories involves the idea of 'natural selection'?

    A the Big Bang theory ☐   **C** evolution ☐

    B the Genesis creation story ☐   **D** religious truth ☐

    (1 mark)

   (b) Give **two** solutions to environmental damage.   **(2 marks)**

....

....

....

....

(c) Explain **two** contrasting beliefs in contemporary British society about animal experimentation. In your answer you should refer to the main religious tradition of Great Britain and one or more other religious traditions. **(4 marks)**

(d) Explain **two** teachings about euthanasia. Refer to scripture or another source of religious beliefs and teachings in your answer. **(5 marks)**

(e) 'Caring for the world should be the most important priority for everyone.' Evaluate this statement. In your answer you:
- should give reasoned arguments in support of this statement
- should give reasoned arguments to support a different point of view
- should refer to religious arguments
- may refer to non-religious arguments
- should reach a justified conclusion. **(12 marks)**

Total: 24 marks

(Example student responses and mark scheme on p. 62)

2   Explain **two** similar religious beliefs about looking after the environment. In your answer you must refer to one or more religious traditions.
(4 marks)

....

....

....

....

Total: 4 marks

(Example student responses and mark scheme on p. 67)

3   Explain **two** different religious beliefs about abortion. In your answer you must refer to one or more religious traditions.
(4 marks)

....

....

....

....

Total: 4 marks

(Example student responses and mark scheme on p. 69)

Theme C: The existence of God and revelation

1   **(a)** Which of these is agnostic?
   A   someone who doesn't believe God exists
   B   someone who believes in God
   C   someone who isn't sure if God exists or not
   D   someone who does not believe in God
(1 mark)

   (b) Give **two** alternative explanations an atheist might give for a claim by someone of special revelation.
(2 marks)

....

....

....

....

(c) Explain **two** contrasting beliefs in contemporary British society about miracles. In your answer you should refer to the main religious tradition of Great Britain and one or more other religious or non-religious beliefs. **(4 marks)**

....

....

....

....

(d) Explain **two** teachings about special revelation. Refer to sacred writings or another source of religious belief and teaching in your answer. **(5 marks)**

....

....

....

....

....

....

(e) 'Science and religion are not compatible when discussing the origins of the universe.'
Evaluate this statement. In your answer you:
- should give reasoned arguments in support of this statement
- should give reasoned arguments to support a different point of view
- should refer to religious arguments
- may refer to non-religious arguments
- should reach a justified conclusion.

(12 marks)

....

....

....

....

....

....

....

....

     AQA GCSE (9–1) Religious Studies A Exam Question Practice

....
....
....

Total: 24 marks

(Example student responses and mark scheme on p. 70)

2   Explain **two** similar beliefs about revelation. In your answer you must refer to one or more religious traditions.   **(4 marks)**

....
....
....

Total: 4 marks

(Example student responses and mark scheme on p. 75)

3   Explain **two** contrasting beliefs about enlightenment as a source of knowledge of the divine. In your answer you must refer to one or more religious traditions.   **(4 marks)**

....
....
....

Total: 4 marks

(Example student responses and mark scheme on p. 76)

Theme D: Religion, peace and conflict

1   **(a)** What is meant by reconciliation?
    A   to take revenge after being invaded or attacked ☐
    B   making up between two groups who have had a disagreement ☐
    C   to pay back for harmful action ☐
    D   a war which involves religion ☐
                          (1 mark)

    (b) Give **two** reasons why nations go to war.   **(2 marks)**

....
....
....

(c) Explain **two** contrasting beliefs in contemporary British society about weapons of mass destruction (WMD). In your answer you should refer to the main religious tradition of Great Britain and one or more other religious traditions.

(4 marks)

(d) Explain **two** teachings about peace. Refer to sacred writings or another source of religious belief and teaching in your answer.

(5 marks)

(e) 'Religion is not a cause of war.' Evaluate this statement. In your answer you:
- should give reasoned arguments in support of this statement
- should give reasoned arguments to support a different point of view
- should refer to religious arguments
- may refer to non-religious arguments
- should reach a justified conclusion.

(12 marks)

....

....

Total: 24 marks

(Example student responses and mark scheme on p. 77)

2   Explain **two** similar religious beliefs about fighting in a war. In your answer you should refer to one or more religious traditions.   **(4 marks)**

....

....

....

Total: 4 marks

(Example student responses and mark scheme on p. 83)

3   Explain **two** contrasting religious beliefs about protest. In your answer you should refer to one or more religious traditions.   **(4 marks)**

....

....

....

Total: 4 marks

(Example student responses and mark scheme on p. 85)

Theme E: Religion, crime and punishment

1   **(a)** Which of the following is the definition for deterrence?
    A   a person's belief about what is right and wrong
    B   a person's desire to make up for their crimes
    C   a voice inside a person's head putting them off doing bad things
    D   an aim of punishment used to put criminals off crime

   (1 mark)

   (b) Give **two** causes of crime.   **(2 marks)**

....

....

....

(c) Explain **two** contrasting beliefs in contemporary British society about the death penalty. In your answer you should refer to the main religious tradition of Great Britain and one or more other religious traditions.

(4 marks)

(d) Explain **two** teachings about where evil comes from. Refer to sacred writings or another source of religious belief and teaching in your answer.

(5 marks)

(e) 'Criminals should always be forgiven rather than punished.' Evaluate this statement. In your answer you:
- should give reasoned arguments in support of this statement
- should give reasoned arguments to support a different point of view
- should refer to religious arguments
- may refer to non-religious arguments
- should reach a justified conclusion.

(12 marks)

Total: 24 marks

(Example student responses and mark scheme on p. 86)

2   Explain **two** similar religious beliefs about reformation as an aim of punishment. In your answer you should refer to one or more religious traditions.   **(4 marks)**

....

....

....

Total: 4 marks

(Example student responses and mark scheme on p. 92)

3   Explain **two** contrasting religious beliefs about where evil comes from. In your answer you should refer to one or more religious traditions.   **(4 marks)**

....

....

....

Total: 4 marks

(Example student responses and mark scheme on p. 93)

Theme F: Religion, human rights and social justice

1   **(a)** Which of the following does not have a responsibility to help the poor?

A government	**C** people traffickers
B charities	**D** religious groups

(1 mark)

   (b) Give **two** human rights in the Declaration of Human Rights.   **(2 marks)**

....

....

   (c) Explain **two** contrasting beliefs in contemporary British society about the status of women. In your answer you should refer to the main religious tradition of Great Britain and one or more other religious traditions.   **(4 marks)**

....

....

....

(d) Explain **two** teachings about tackling poverty. Refer to sacred writings or another source of religious belief and teaching in your answer. **(5 marks)**

(e) 'It is wrong to be wealthy in the world today.' Evaluate this statement. In your answer you:
- should give reasoned arguments in support of this statement
- should give reasoned arguments to support a different point of view
- should refer to religious arguments
- may refer to non-religious arguments
- should reach a justified conclusion. **(12 marks)**

Total: 24 marks

(Example student responses and mark scheme on p. 94)

2 Explain **two** similar beliefs about giving to charity. In your answer you should refer to one or more religious traditions. **(4 marks)**

Total: 4 marks

(Example student responses and mark scheme on p. 100)

3   Explain **two** contrasting religious beliefs about giving to the poor. In your answer you should refer to one or more religious traditions.

(4 marks)

Total: 4 marks

(Example student responses and mark scheme on p. 101)

Paper 2A Thematic Studies Sample set 2

Theme A: Relationships and families

1   (a) Which of these describes a homosexual relationship?

   A   a relationship between a man and a woman

   B   a relationship between two men

   C   a relationship where a man has more than one wife

   D   a relationship where a woman has more than one husband

(1 mark)

   (b) Give **two** reasons people get married.

(2 marks)

   (c) Explain **two** contrasting beliefs in contemporary British society about contraception. In your answer you should refer to the main religious tradition of Great Britain and one or more other religious traditions.

(4 marks)

(d) Explain **two** teachings about gender discrimination. Refer to sacred writings or another source of religious belief and teaching in your answer. **(5 marks)**

....

....

....

....

....

(e) 'Only married heterosexual couples should have children.' Evaluate this statement. In your answer you:
> should give reasoned arguments in support of this statement
> should give reasoned arguments to support a different point of view
> should refer to religious arguments
> may refer to non-religious arguments
> should reach a justified conclusion. **(12 marks)**

....

....

....

....

....

....

....

....

....

....

....

....

Total: 24 marks

(Example student responses and mark scheme on p. 102)

  AQA GCSE (9–1) Religious Studies A Exam Question Practice

Theme B: Religion and life

1 **(a)** What is meant by sustainable development?

    A the continual use of fossil fuels for the future ☐

    B new technological developments should all be infinite or long-lasting ☐

    C to try and protect an area of nature for the long term ☐

    D natural resources are being used in greater quantities and at a faster rate than at any time in history ☐

(1 mark)

(b) Give **two** effects of pollution. **(2 marks)**

....

....

(c) Explain **two** contrasting beliefs in contemporary British society about abortion. In your answer you should refer to the main religious tradition of Great Britain and one or more other religious traditions. **(4 marks)**

....

....

....

....

....

....

(d) Explain **two** teachings about why religious people should look after the environment. Refer to sacred writings or another source of religious belief and teaching in your answer. **(5 marks)**

....

....

....

....

....

....

....

....

(e) 'Hospices mean that there is no need for euthanasia.' Evaluate this statement. In your answer you:

➢ should give reasoned arguments in support of this statement
➢ should give reasoned arguments to support a different point of view
➢ should refer to religious arguments
➢ may refer to non-religious arguments
➢ should reach a justified conclusion.

(12 marks)

Total: 24 marks

(Example student responses and mark scheme on p. 107)

Theme C: The existence of God and revelation

1 **(a)** Which of the following is not usually used as an argument for the existence of God?

A first cause ☐   **C** science ☐
B design ☐   **D** miracles ☐

(1 mark)

(b) Give **two** reasons why some people say God exists.

(2 marks)

(c) Explain **two** contrasting beliefs in contemporary British society about nature as general revelation. In your answer you should refer to the main religious tradition of Great Britain and one or more non-religious beliefs. **(4 marks)**

(d) Explain **two** teachings about the nature of God. Refer to sacred writings or another source of religious belief and teaching in your answer. **(5 marks)**

(e) 'The argument from miracles proves God existence.' Evaluate this statement. In your answer you:
- should give reasoned arguments in support of this statement
- should give reasoned arguments to support a different point of view
- should refer to religious arguments
- may refer to non-religious arguments
- should reach a justified conclusion. **(12 marks)**

Total: 24 marks

(Example student responses and mark scheme on p. 113)

Theme D: Religion, peace and conflict

1   **(a)** What is meant by forgiveness?

     A not to blame someone any more for the wrongs they have done ☐

     B to forget a wrong action done to a person ☐

     C a religious idea to prevent war ☐

     D the belief that war should never be fought ☐

                              (1 mark)

   (b) Give **two** consequences of war.   **(2 marks)**

   (c) Explain **two** contrasting beliefs in contemporary British society about violence. In your answer you should refer to the main religious tradition of Great Britain and one or more other religious traditions.   **(4 marks)**

   (d) Explain **two** teachings about terrorism. Refer to sacred writings or another source of religious belief and teaching in your answer.   **(5 marks)**

(e) 'Everyone who is religious should be a pacifist.' Evaluate this statement. In your answer you:
  - should give reasoned arguments in support of this statement
  - should give reasoned arguments to support a different point of view
  - should refer to religious arguments
  - may refer to non-religious arguments
  - should reach a justified conclusion. **(12 marks)**

Total: 24 marks

(Example student responses and mark scheme on p. 118)

Theme E: Religion, crime and punishment

1   **(a)** Which of the following is a definition of retribution?
   A   to work with criminals to be able to turn their lives around
   B   to make the punishment fit the crime so it almost seems like an act of revenge
   C   to make up for the crime that was committed – to repair the damage
   D   to ensure the criminal has the toughest punishment available
   (1 mark)

   (b) Give **two** ways in which victim support can offer help to victims of crime.   **(2 marks)**

(c) Explain **two** contrasting beliefs in contemporary British society about corporal punishment. In your answer you should refer to the main religious tradition of Great Britain and one or more other religious traditions. **(4 marks)**

....

....

....

(d) Explain **two** teachings about following the law. Refer to sacred writings or another source of religious belief and teaching in your answer. **(5 marks)**

....

....

....

....

....

(e) 'Prison is better than other forms of punishment for all criminals.' Evaluate this statement. In your answer you:
- should give reasoned arguments in support of this statement
- should give reasoned arguments to support a different point of view
- should refer to religious arguments
- may refer to non-religious arguments
- should reach a justified conclusion. **(12 marks)**

....

....

....

....

....

....

....

Total: 24 marks

(Example student responses and mark scheme on p. 124)

Theme F: Religion, human rights and social justice

1   **(a)** Which of the following is a religious charity helping the poor in Britain?

    A Salvation Army ☐   **C** Save the Children ☐

    B Shelter ☐   **D** RSPCA ☐

    (1 mark)

  (b) Give **two** reasons people may be prejudiced. **(2 marks)**

  (c) Explain **two** contrasting beliefs in contemporary British society about freedom of religious expression. In your answer you should refer to the main religious tradition of Great Britain and one or more other religious traditions. **(4 marks)**

  (d) Explain **two** teachings about racism. Refer to sacred writings or another source of religious belief and teaching in your answer. **(5 marks)**

(e) 'Poverty is the greatest problem facing religious people today.' Evaluate this statement. In your answer you:
> should give reasoned arguments in support of this statement
> should give reasoned arguments to support a different point of view
> should refer to religious arguments
> may refer to non-religious arguments
> should reach a justified conclusion.

(12 marks)

Total: 24 marks

(Example student responses and mark scheme on p. 129)

EXAMPLE RESPONSES AND MARK SCHEMES

The student responses

This section shows sample answers from two students. One set (A) is strong, the other (B) weaker. The answers are followed by expert comments (shown by the icon **e**) that indicate where credit is due. In the weaker answers, they also point out areas for improvement, specific problems and common errors. In some instances, 'Muhammad' is followed by '(pbuh)'. This stands for '(peace be upon him)'.

Paper 1 The study of religions: beliefs, teachings and practices

Christianity

Question 1
Student A

(a) B: God

e **Correct.   1 mark**

(b) omnipotent, just

e **Two clear ideas. There is no need to waste time writing in a sentence as the question says 'give' – here meaning 'list'.   2 marks**

(c) First, the idea that God was willing to send his Son to earth to live with us shows Christians how much God loves us and therefore how much we should love him in our lives. Our worship, prayer and praise should show that great love. Second, that the love God showed us, by sending his Son, is an example for us to follow. It was selfless and we should do the same, for example like Mother Teresa did in her life.

e **Good structure – offers the examiner two clear ideas, each with an explanation. The development of both ideas demonstrates the 'influence' each should have in the life of a Christian.   4 marks**

(d) The first teaching is that in the Bible it says 'God so loved the world that he gave his only son so that we should have eternal life'. For Christians, salvation comes through the death and resurrection of Jesus – he was born into the world and overcame death so that Christians can have eternal life with God.

The second teaching is that Jesus said 'Whoever believes in me shall have eternal life'. Jesus is teaching that entry into heaven is not about following the law like the Jews were obsessed with but by believing in God, living in the right way and having the right thoughts in our minds and love in our hearts for God and everyone.

(e) **Good structure – this answer offers the examiner two clear ideas, each with an explanation of the meaning of the teaching to Christians.   5 marks**

(e) There are many Christians who do actually believe that the creation story is true – that it all happened as the Bible describes. The writers were directly inspired by God so it has to be the truth. When they say the truth they mean that the world was created from nothing and that what it says happened on each day happened as a fact. This interpretation is called a literal interpretation. These Christians also believe that there is one clear message that God was responsible for all creation in 6 days, he rested on the 7th Day and that he was pleased with his work. They also believe that human beings were created in God's image and were given authority and responsibility over all of creation as the most intelligent. Many people find this hard to believe because there are mistakes in the logical order, e.g. the sun and moon didn't happen until after day 1, yet on day 1 there was light and dark. Others have an issue with it being done in 7 days, especially with the science and evolution ideas.

Other Christians believe that it is the message of Genesis that is important. It is not important whether day 1 actually happened as it literally states. What matters is the message that God did create from nothing. The world is an ordered, interdependent world – made by a plan rather than by chance. From the story we learn that to be human gives us potential and that because we are made in the image of God we are all equal and all have value. We do also have responsibility, which is a privilege, so being a steward is part of the task God has given us. Many of the literal Christians agree with these ideas but still believe that the Bible is a true account.

(e) **The arguments in this paragraph could be developed a bit more.**

In conclusion I think that it all depends on what the question means by 'truth'. Do we mean the truth of how it actually happened or do we mean the truth as in its meaning? Creation is an unanswerable question so to say ALL Christians should believe in the story as true is far too definite. There are different ways to understand it, but what is important is the message that however it was done, it was a result of the work of God.

(e) **Good structure – this answer gives clear, logical arguments and views and attempts some evaluation of each point. The conclusion brings everything together to address the question fully.   L4: 11 marks**

Question 1
Student B

(a) Father, Son, Holy Spirit

(e) **Incorrect. The correct answer is B: God. Be careful to read the question carefully as it could ask you what something IS or what it IS NOT.   0 marks**

(b) Oneness of God and the fact that God can do anything.

(e) **The oneness of God is associated with the Trinity but this answer would get 1 mark. The second idea is a *description* of God rather than a *characteristic* (i.e. omnipotent / all powerful). No mark can be given for this as the examiner has to try to interpret what the student means. 1 mark**

(c) Incarnation means that Jesus came to earth as a human like us. This shows how much God loves us and that we should love God.

(e) **The opening sentence is a definition not an explanation. The stated influence on Christian life – that because God loved us so Christians should love him – is too simple as it does not include *how* Christians show this love in their lives.**

Some people like Mother Teresa have lived their lives showing love for God.

(e) **The second part mentions an influence but lacks a link to the incarnation, e.g. Mother Theresa lived her life trying to follow the selfless love shown by God in sending his son to earth.   2 marks**

(d) For Christians, salvation comes through the death and resurrection of Jesus – he overcame death so that Christians can have eternal life. In the Bible it says God so loved the world that he gave his only son so that we should have eternal life.

(e) **This answer does not clearly explain TWO teachings. The first sentence explains a teaching about the source of salvation, and develops this. The second sentence could be seen either as a separate point or a further extension of the first explanation.   3 marks**

(e) Most Christians would disagree with this statement because it can't possibly have happened in 7 days. Given what we know now about how the world and life develops, things just being placed on earth doesn't make sense to us. Humans didn't just exist, they evolved as did all the other species and also there are mistakes in the order of how the writer tells us what happened. Light and darkness before the sun and moon. These Christians believe it is the message of the story that is important. The myth gives us a message because the writer wasn't there right at the beginning so how could he know what exactly happened? The message we need to understand is that God was responsible for creation, humans were created in his image and we now have a responsibility as stewards to look after it.

Other Christians would say that all Christians should believe it as the truth because it is written in the Bible and as it was written by God it has to be true. God is all-powerful so he can do anything even if it is beyond our understanding.

(e) **Argument lacks depth and range of ideas.**

There are many different ideas about creation and to say that all Christians should believe it as true is a bit strong. We will never know and whether it happened as the Bible says or not, as long as Christians believe it was God that was responsible, that is all that matters.

(e) **This answer attempts to develop arguments from both points of view but is weak in places. The first paragraph on other views is the stronger one, offering relevant knowledge and some attempt at evaluation. Some of it reads a little too much like AO1 rather than AO2 evaluation. The conclusion is simple but clear.   L3: 8 marks**

Mark scheme

1 **(a)** 1 mark for the correct answer.

The correct answer is B: God

Hints and tips

These questions usually rely entirely on knowledge of key words and terms – you need to learn them.

Be careful to read the question carefully as it could ask you what something IS or what it IS NOT.

(b) 1 mark per correct answer, up to 2 marks maximum.

Answers might include:

omnipotent (all-powerful), all-loving (omnibenevolent), all knowing (omniscient), just, Father, creator, forgiver

Hints and tips

Do not explain anything unless instructed to – just give two words or phrases to answer this question. That frees up your time to answer later questions.

(c) Total of 4 marks.

For the first way given:

– a **simple** explanation of a relevant and accurate point which shows the influence of the belief **(1 mark)**

– a **detailed** explanation of a relevant and accurate point which shows the influence of the belief **(2 marks)**

For the second way given:

– a **simple** explanation of a relevant and accurate point which shows the influence of the belief **(1 mark)**

– a **detailed** explanation of a relevant and accurate point which shows the influence of the belief **(2 marks)**

Answers might include:

The incarnation shows Christians how loving God is in sending his Son to become mortal – so Christians are inspired to show love to God in return through their lives.

It shows Christians how much of a sacrifice God made to send his only Son – so Christians sacrifice time to show their love – through worship, prayer, praise and living their lives well.

It shows God's selfless love and commitment to humanity, so Christians try and show this kind of love to others – which is often selfless – by giving up important things in life for the sake of others, Mother Teresa being the perfect example.

Hints and tips

You have to give two **different** ideas – only writing about one way in which beliefs/teachings influence believers is worth a maximum of 2 marks.

Try to make sure you are developing your ideas, not just writing lists of new ideas.

When the question asks you to explain how a belief/teaching **influences** a believer, it is asking for the impact on someone's life – what difference it makes to them and the way they live/behave.

(d) Total of 4 marks + 1 mark

Look for explanation of two different teachings in the answer.

For the first teaching given:

– a **simple** explanation of a teaching which is both clearly relevant to the question and accurate **(1 mark)**

– a **detailed** explanation of a teaching which is both clearly relevant to the question and accurate **(2 marks)**

For the second teaching given:

– a **simple** explanation of a teaching which is both clearly relevant to the question and accurate **(1 mark)**

– a **detailed** explanation of a teaching which is both clearly relevant to the question and accurate **(2 marks)**

A relevant and accurate reference to scripture and/or sacred writing has been given. **(1 mark)**

Answers might include:

'God so loved the world that He gave His only Son so that we should have eternal life' – Jesus' death is a clear part of God's plan for salvation.

'Whoever believes in me shall have eternal life' – Jesus is showing that salvation is about belief in him, which contradicts the Jewish idea of salvation through following all parts of the law.

Answers may reference the terms 'salvation through works' (salvation can be earned) and 'the death of Jesus as atonement for sin' (salvation is only possible because Jesus took on the sins of humanity to reconcile it with God).

Hints and tips

You have to explain two different teachings in the answer to this question.

The mark scheme tells you that the points have to be 'clearly relevant' – if you read (or write) something that does not make sense, or that you have to think about to make it relevant, then it is not a good answer.

A good way to answer is to give a teaching and then say how that teaching applies to the question. Then explain the point you are making (rather than adding a teaching at the end of the answer).

Try to structure your answer so that it is easy for the examiner to identify your two teachings. For example, begin your first paragraph with something like 'The first teaching is…'. Begin a subsequent paragraph with 'The second teaching is…'. Each teaching needs more explanation added to it.

Remember teachings do not always have to be direct quotes from the Bible – check the mark scheme.

(e) These questions are marked according to levels of response – this means your answer is judged for its quality overall, not for how many different arguments you present.

Answers might include:

Arguments in support of the view:

- *The Bible is the word of God so everything in it is true.*
- *God is all powerful so even things we do not understand can be true.*
- *God is beyond understanding so we should just accept the story as true.*
- *If all Christians accept the creation is true it unites the faith.*

Arguments supporting other views:

- *The story is not logical for the modern mind in terms of what we know now.*
- *Because of what science tells us about the development of life, the creation cannot be true.*
- *The story is a myth so it is the message that matters not the truth of how it happened.*
- *Depends what is meant by 'true' – historically accurate or accurate in meaning.*
- *We just do not know enough to accept that it is true – too long ago.*
- *The Bible can mean different things to different people so it is not possible for all to believe the same things.*

Levels mark scheme

The following applies to all sections.

Levels	Criteria	Marks
4	A well-argued response, reasoned consideration of different points of view. This means that a series of arguments are presented which are well explained as well as supported by relevant evidence/information. These arguments are logical in their presentation, so the examiner can see good sense in them and does not have to think about what may or may not be meant.	10–12
3	Reasoned consideration of different points of view. This means that more than one point of view is presented. There are several arguments on each side, which are explained and supported by evidence/information. The examiner can see the relevance, but it is not as clearly obvious as in Level 4.	7–9
2	Reasoned consideration of a point of view. This means that just one point of view has been argued, even if it is strongly supported by relevant evidence/information. The mark will increase depending on how many arguments are used in support. OR The answer has more than one point of view, but the supporting evidence for each is limited. There is only limited development of the arguments.	4–6
1	Point of view with reason(s) stated in support. This means that a series of reasons are given to support one point of view. There is no development/explanation.	1–3
0	Nothing worthy of credit. This means there is nothing right about this answer.	0

Hints and tips

You need to make sure you give arguments to agree **and** to disagree with the statement – if you give only one point of view, then you cannot get above half marks.

Your answer must be full of religious content – this is a statement about religious beliefs and teachings.

The top level requires good development of the arguments you present. This means giving the argument and explaining clearly why it supports/contradicts the statement using detailed examples. This level is looking for a lot of development.

Try to get into the habit of offering three 'for' and three 'against' arguments in all your AO2 answers. Explain and provide examples for each, and include teachings if possible – this will help push your response to a higher level.

Question 2

Student A

(a)   D: Easter

🄮   **Correct.   1 mark**

(b)   Liturgical, non-liturgical

🄮   **Two clear, correct answers.   2 marks**

(c)   Set prayers are prayers that are said each week in a church service. This is done so that the congregation can learn them and join in or repeat them at home too. The Lord's Prayer or the Grace are examples of set prayers. Liturgical forms of worship found in the Roman Catholic or Orthodox churches use set prayers. Many people like such prayers because it is often hard to think what you want to say to God.

There are informal prayers too where the words come more from the individual's heart. They are spontaneous and mean more because they can be more personal. With these prayers you aren't just repeating words and phrases. Less formal services include a lot of these. Many Protestant services use informal prayer.

🄮   **Two clear, contrasting prayer types identified and explained well, using one paragraph for each type which makes it very clear for the examiner to see.   4 marks**

(d)   The Bible tells Christians to 'love their neighbour' and Christians show this by helping people in their local communities. Today there is a big problem in Britain because of the recession and the price of food. Many people do not earn enough to feed their families. Food banks see people donate food and volunteers sort it and deliver it to families in need of help. Many people are referred by social services and are given vouchers to exchange for a balanced assortment of food.

Another way Christians help in the community is by becoming street pastors. These people are men and women called to help others and go out on the streets at weekend to help care for the needs of young people who may get themselves into difficult situations because of drink or drugs. They are there to listen and not to judge. The Bible says 'do not judge' and 'to treat others as we wish to be treated'. We have all been in need of help rather than judgement at some point in our lives.

🄮   **Two clear responses and clear teachings shown in action. Obvious development shown in both parts.   5 marks**

(e) Some Christians would disagree with this statement for many reasons. The Bible does not distinguish between which poor should be helped, just that they should be. Jesus taught us to 'love our neighbours', which means anyone, and also from the parable of the sheep and goats that any help given to those in need would be as if we were helping God himself. Jesus himself helped some of the most in need in society – those who were total outcasts like lepers. If we look at the world today, we could easily argue that the needs of those in developing countries are far greater than the needs of people here. However others might say that their needs are so great and that we have been helping them for so long and still there has been little improvement so we are wasting our money. It will take millions to help the people of Africa, for example, but millions here would do far more because the problem isn't as big. Alternatively, though, a small donation like £5 would feed an African family far longer than it would in the UK.

Also much of their poverty is not their fault or due to the wrong choices they made but more about to the circumstances they find themselves in and things they can do nothing about like the climate. In the UK it could be argued there is no real reason for people to be poor if they approach life in the right way and so they don't deserve the help as much.

Jesus said that it was those who were sick that were in need of a doctor – but he didn't specify the place, so we should help as many as we can and the needs outside Britain are far greater. Conversely we cannot ignore the needs of those closest to us as it's on our doorstep so to speak, a bit like Lazarus at the gates of the rich man. Surely our duty is to help where we actually see it. We should put our own country right before helping others.

In conclusion religion is worldwide and so we should help all those who need help where we can. It is true that things like disease, hunger, malnutrition and living conditions are nowhere near as bad in the UK as in some other countries, so their need is far greater. We should deal with the worst and most helpless first and then hopefully one day they will become self-sufficient and won't need our help. Many people here are in a better position to help themselves, but still need guiding in the right direction.

e **Excellent structure with evaluation given throughout; each point discussed against another. Good application of teachings and a clear and justified conclusion.   L4: 12 marks**

Question 2
Student B

(a) Christmas, Good Friday, Lent

e **Incorrect. The correct answer is D: Easter. Be careful to read the question carefully as it could ask you what something IS or what it IS NOT.   0 marks**

(b) Private worship

e **Correct answer   1 mark**

the one where there is no set pattern

e **The second answer is more a definition of non-liturgical rather than a statement of the form – a generous examiner might give the benefit here but it is a good lesson to learn: don't make the examiner try to guess what you mean.   1 mark**

(c) The first contrasting type is set prayers repeated by the worshippers each week so that they become familiar in the services. It also means people can join in. Many have been written by famous Christians in the past so are really well known. Roman Catholics use these a lot.

The second contrasting prayer is like the Lord's Prayer as it comes from the Bible. This is used in all types of Christian churches.

(e) **The first paragraph identifies the type of prayer and then develops the answer but the second part is incorrect, as in fact the Lord's Prayer is an example of a set prayer.   2 marks**

(d) Food banks dish out food to those in the community who cannot afford to feed their families as Christians should help others.

Street pastors work in cities and towns at weekends. They help young people who might have had too much to drink out clubbing. They believe it's their Christian duty.

(e) **Two ways have been identified, both in a simple way. There is little development of either answer, so 1 mark for each. Vague reference to Christian duty is not quite enough for the 1 mark available for relevant teaching; further explanation of the way in which this duty is expressed in community service is needed.   2 marks**

(e) I disagree with this because the needs of people in Africa are far greater than the people here. They have absolutely nothing – no food, water, education, healthcare or shelter – what we would call the basic things needed to survive. Many are in the middle of war zones and live in fear daily. Some are forced to leave their homes as refugees. Children are dying daily of things like malaria when in a modern world this shouldn't happen. The most important thing is that no matter how much they want to help themselves, they can't because the circumstances won't allow them to. It's not their fault they were born into poverty caused by climate where it's too hot and dry, or too cold and wet, is it? They deserve our help more than anyone.

In the UK there are all the opportunities available to make a success of life but some people choose not to take them. We all have a free education, healthcare, food and clean water but some people choose the wrong way and aren't willing to put any effort into life to get what they need. There is also the benefits system that already helps poor people.

Jesus helped those in society who suffered the most so we should too.

(e) **A strong range of ideas which are supported well and there is an attempt to bring in religious teachings. However all the arguments are on one side of the debate only and therefore marking cannot go beyond level 2. Make quite sure you have read the instructions of the question – here both sides of the argument are required.   L2: 6 marks**

Mark scheme

2   (a) 1 mark for the correct answer.
The correct answer is D: Easter

Hints and tips

These questions usually rely entirely on knowledge of key words and terms – you need to learn them.

Be careful to read the question carefully as it could ask you what something IS or what it IS NOT.

(b) 1 mark per correct answer, up to 2 marks maximum.

Answers might include:

liturgical, non-liturgical, informal or private worship.

Hints and tips

Do not explain anything unless instructed to – just give two words or phrases to answer this question. That frees up your time to answer later questions.

(c) Total of 4 marks.

For the first way given:
- a **simple** explanation of a way in which Christians use prayer (1 mark)
- a **detailed** explanation of a way in which Christians use prayer (2 marks)

For the second way given:
- a **simple** explanation of a contrasting way in which Christians use prayer (1 mark)
- a **detailed** explanation of a contrasting way in which Christians use prayer (2 marks)

Answers might include:

Set prayers: The Lord's Prayer, prayers from the Book of Common Prayer, Book of Psalms, formal written prayers, liturgical prayers, seasonal prayers.

Informal prayer: non-liturgical prayer, individual prayer, prayer at home, charismatic prayer, meditational prayer.

Hints and tips

You have to give two different elements when asked for contrast – only writing about one element is worth a maximum of 2 marks.

Try to make sure you are developing your ideas, not just writing lists of new ideas.

(d) Total of 4 marks + 1 mark

Look for explanation of two different ways in which Christians work in the community in the answer.

For the first example given:
- a **simple** explanation which is both clearly relevant to the question and accurate (1 mark)
- a **detailed** explanation which is both clearly relevant to the question and accurate (2 marks)

For the second example given:
- a **simple** explanation which is both clearly relevant to the question and accurate (1 mark)
- a **detailed** explanation which is both clearly relevant to the question and accurate (2 marks)

A relevant and accurate reference to scripture and/or sacred writing has been given. (1 mark)

Answers might include:

Food banks; street pastors; youth groups to support young people; counselling and pastoral support services; community outreach work; church growth through New Expressions, etc; working in schools, hospitals and prisons to give spiritual guidance.

The parable of the sheep and goats – whosoever helped one of them has helped me (Jesus) is a good teaching for all of these; also Jesus' example of helping those in need during his ministry ('What would Jesus do'); Love thy neighbour; 'Go and make disciples of all nations, etc.'

Answers may reference the terms 'salvation through works' (salvation can be earned) and 'the death of Jesus as atonement for sin' (salvation is only possible because Jesus took on the sins of humanity to reconcile it with God). Where a relevant and accurate reference to scripture and/or sacred writing has been given, award 1 mark.

Hints and tips

You have to explain two different ways of working in the community in the answer to this question.

The mark scheme tells you that the points have to be 'clearly relevant' – if you write something that does not make sense, or that you have to think about to make it relevant, then it is not a good answer.

A good way to answer is to give a way Christians work in the community, and then explain how this relates to Christian teaching.

(e) These questions are marked according to levels of response – this means your answer is judged for its quality overall, not for how many different arguments you present.

Answers might include:

Arguments in support of the view:

➤ *Story of Lazarus at the rich man's gate – we should help those we see.*
➤ *It is not such a massive problem so easier and cheaper to help.*
➤ *If we can not help our own how can we help others?*
➤ *If we help our own society it makes our society better and safer to live in.*

Arguments supporting other views:

➤ *People in other countries have far greater need – they are in abject poverty whereas in the UK they are not.*
➤ *People outside the UK cannot help themselves and the fault of being in poverty is not their own – climate, war, debt etc. whereas fault maybe can be attributed to some of the poor in the UK.*
➤ *The Bible teachings to help all – 'love neighbour', 'what is done for others is done for me'.*
➤ *A small amount goes a long way.*
➤ *Jesus often helped the most needy in society so Christians should follow the example.*
➤ *There are other groups like the government to help in the UK.*

Hints and tips

You need to make sure you give arguments to agree and to disagree with the statement – if you give only one point of view, then you cannot get above half marks.

Your answer must be full of religious content – this is a statement about religious beliefs and teachings.

The top level requires good development of the arguments you present. This means giving the argument and explaining clearly why it supports/contradicts the statement using detailed examples. This level is looking for a lot of development.

Try to get into the habit of offering three for and three against arguments in all your AO2 answers. Explain and provide examples for each, and include teachings if possible – this will help push your response to a higher level.

Islam

Question 1

Student A

(a) D: Five Pillars

(e) **The Five Pillars are the core foundations of the religion, not one of the Six Articles.   1 mark**

(b) immanent, transcendent

(e) **Two clear correct qualities.   2 marks**

(c) Belief in angels influences Muslims because firstly they believe that there are angels who are watching over them recording their every action so that on Judgement Day their book can be opened and read. As this determines a place in paradise, Muslims are careful to make sure they do more good deeds than bad deeds.

Second, Muslims believe there are guardian angels like Hafaza who watch over them until the time of their death. This makes them feel like they are protected and loved in their daily lives.

(e) **Two clear influences given – two types of angels identified, what the angels do and how they influence Muslims today.   4 marks**

(d) In the Qur'an it says 'He is Allah, One.' This is what Tawhid means, oneness. Allah is indivisible, almighty and absolute. He is the ultimate source of creation because he is eternal and everlasting which means he pre-exists everything so not born like humans. He is simply One.

The Qur'an also says 'there is no equivalent to him' meaning that Muslims cannot liken anything to him. If they do they commit the sin of Shirk so, for example, Jesus could not have been the Son of God because no one can have the power of God, so instead Muslims see Jesus as a Prophet.

(e) **The student offers two clearly explained teachings. In fact there are many clearly explained teachings in this answer. The quotations are excellent – though key ideas like 'almighty' and 'absolute' could be taken as quotations as well.   5 marks**

(e) The Qur'an is the ultimate book of guidance given through Jibril to Muhammad (pbuh). It is the direct word of Allah and covers all aspects of life. As it comes from Allah there are no mistakes, 'Falsehood shall never come to it', whereas there might have been in other books or from the words of the prophets. So it has to be the main source of guidance. Anything about any aspect of life can be found in the Qur'an. It covers the basics of worship and contains the laws of Allah. It contains details of how the world began and answers Muslims' questions about what happens when they die. It covers issues of birth, marriage, death and provides spiritual guidance for all life's situations and difficulties. So if it covers everything why would any other source of guidance be needed? Other responses might be though that the book is very old and does not contain teachings on the kinds of issues we face in the twenty-first century so it is difficult to seek guidance from the Qur'an. Also many cannot understand the language it is written in and the way it is written. If it then has to be interpreted, this might distort the message.

Many Muslims would say that the Qur'an forms part of their source of guidance rather than it being the only source needed. For example Muhammad (pbuh) left his Sunnah and his life as an example and sometimes it is easier to follow a human being than a book. The prophet was sent to 'instruct you in scripture and wisdom and new knowledge' so his guidance must be necessary. Also Muhammad (pbuh) had done the interpretation for himself and as the last prophet Muslims feel his interpretation is correct. However in response to this Muslims might say that Muhammad (pbuh) is no longer with us and that is an issue, whereas the Qur'an is here with them all the time.

There are also those who believe that we need more than just the Qur'an, for example religious leaders or Imams in the Shi'a tradition. They are inspired by Allah to guide Muslims in their daily lives, and sometimes it is better to get guidance from someone you can talk to than from reading a book. Also when reading and interpreting the Qur'an how can Muslims know they have the correct interpretation?

To conclude Muslims generally require more than just the Qur'an for guidance. Yes it is the ultimate guide but on its own it isn't enough. They are better guided with a combination of the Qur'an, the Sunnah and religious teachers today.

ⓔ Well-structured, clear ideas are given here. Each idea is evaluated and there is a logical conclusion. This answer keeps referring back to the statement in the question which means it stays focussed. This is a useful example to follow. L4: 12 marks

Question 1
Student B

(a) Angels, Holy Books, Judgement Day

ⓔ Incorrect. The correct answer is D: Five Pillars. Be careful to read the question carefully as it could ask you what something IS or what it IS NOT. 0 marks

(b) Beneficent which means that Allah is kind and compassionate.

ⓔ This is a correct characteristic. The second half of the answer simply explains the characteristic. No second characteristic is stated. 1 mark

(c) Angels are all around Muslims and they have all kinds of roles. Jibril is the most famous as he delivered the Qur'an. He has also seen heaven and hell and tells Muslims heaven is very very hard to get into. This makes Muslims want to improve their behaviour so they have a better chance of making it there.

ⓔ This first paragraph contains some irrelevant material like Jibril delivering the Qur'an, although it does talk about Jibril's seeing heaven and hell and how that influences action.

Mika'il is a good Angel because he provides for human needs. He provides spiritual help for the soul and physical help for the body.

ⓔ The second paragraph is correct in detail but does not relate to any influence. 2 marks

(d) Tawhid means the Oneness of Allah so God cannot be split up into parts. Allah is also not born and does not die so he is eternal and everlasting.

ⓔ There are two ideas about teachings within this answer but both are very simply stated – 'Oneness of Allah' and 'not born and does not die'. There is little if any explanation. The reference to 'Oneness of Allah' is in fact, arguably, not sufficient to gain the mark for quotation; it would have been better to quote – 'He is Allah, One' so the benefit of the doubt is not given here.   **2 marks**

(e) The Qur'an is the direct word of Allah and contains everything Muslims needs to know. Anything about any aspect of life can be found in the Qur'an. It covers the basics of worship and contains the laws of Allah so we know what is right and wrong. It contains details of how the world began and answers Muslims' questions about what happens when they die. It covers issues of birth, marriage, death and provides spiritual guidance for all life's situations and difficulties. So as it covers everything I agree with the statement

Others would disagree though because the Qur'an is not the easiest book to understand so they need religious leaders to help them. That is the point of having Imams at the mosques and sermons to teach people. Also it is much easier to seek guidance from a person, someone you can actually talk to than a book. Also they have Prophet Muhammad (pbuh) as an example. He put the teachings of the Qur'an into action in his life and left teachings for us. This is called the Sunnah and as a Muslim I know quite often that my family look at the Sunnah more than the Qur'an because they understand it better.

I think that all forms of guidance are needed – books and people, and also the Qur'an may not cover some of our modern-day problems so we need other sources too.

ⓔ This is a good response, as both sides of the argument are presented. However it is more one sided than it should be. There is an attempt at evaluation of each point, but this answer lacks the complexity of Student A's response. Islamic teaching is inferred rather than stated.   **L3: 9 marks**

Mark scheme

1   **(a)** 1 mark for the correct answer.
     The correct answer is D: Five Pillars

Hints and tips

These questions usually rely entirely on knowledge of key words and terms – you need to learn them.

Be careful to read the question carefully as it could ask you what something IS or what it IS NOT.

(b) 1 mark per correct answer, up to 2 marks maximum.
     Answers might include:
     oneness, omnipotence, immanent, transcendent, beneficent, merciful, fair and just

Hints and tips

Do not explain anything unless instructed to – just give two words or phrases to answer this question. That frees up your time to answer later questions.

(c) Total of 4 marks.

For the first way given:
- a **simple** explanation of a relevant and accurate point which shows the influence of the belief **(1 mark)**
- a **detailed** explanation of a relevant and accurate point which shows the influence of the belief **(2 marks)**

For the second way given:
- a **simple** explanation of a relevant and accurate point which shows the influence of the belief **(1 mark)**
- a **detailed** explanation of a relevant and accurate point which shows the influence of the belief **(2 marks)**

Answers might include:

Angels watch over Muslims, recording their actions and so they influence behaviour. Angels tell of heaven and hell, so Muslims know how hard it is to enter heaven. Angels look over people like a guardian, so Muslims feel protected and loved. Angels deliver messages from Allah so Muslims know they are true – the Qur'an is then seen as the word of God.

Hints and tips

You have to give two **different** ideas – only writing about one way in which beliefs/teachings influence believers is worth a maximum of 2 marks.

Try to make sure you are developing your ideas, not just writing lists of new ideas.

When the question asks you to explain how the belief/teaching **influences** a believer, the question is asking for the impact on someone's life – what difference it makes to them and the way they live/behave.

(d) Total of 4 marks + 1 mark

Look for explanation of two different teachings in the answer.

For the first teaching given:
- a **simple** explanation of a teaching which is both clearly relevant to the question and accurate **(1 mark)**
- a **detailed** explanation of a teaching which is both clearly relevant to the question and accurate **(2 marks)**

For the second teaching given:
- a **simple** explanation of a teaching which is both clearly relevant to the question and accurate **(1 mark)**
- a **detailed** explanation of a teaching which is both clearly relevant to the question and accurate **(2 marks)**

A relevant and accurate reference to scripture and/or sacred writing has been given. **(1 mark)**

Answers might include:

He is Allah, One, he neither is born or dies, nothing is equivalent to him, indivisible, absolute, beyond understanding, everything belongs to him, he has ultimate power and knowledge.

Hints and tips

You have to explain two **different** teachings in the answer to this question.

The mark scheme tells you that the points have to be 'clearly relevant' – if you read (or write) something that does not make sense, or that you have to think about to make it relevant, then it is not a good answer.

A good way to answer is to give a teaching, and then say how that teaching applies to the question. Then explain the point you are making (rather than adding a teaching at the end of the answer)

Try to structure your answer so that it is easy for the examiner to identify your two teachings. For example, begin your first paragraph with something like 'The first teaching is…'. Begin a subsequent paragraph with 'The second teaching is…'. Each teaching needs more explanation added to it.

Remember teachings do not always have to be direct quotes – check the mark scheme.

(e) These questions are marked according to levels of response – this means your answer is judged for its quality overall, not for how many different arguments you present.

Answers might include:

Arguments in support of the views:

➤ *The Qur'an is the ultimate book of guidance so what else is required.*
➤ *It is the word of Allah so nothing else matters.*
➤ *It contains teachings on all aspects of life.*
➤ *Reference to Qur'an 41:42.*

Arguments supporting other views:

➤ *What about the teachings of Muhammad who the Qur'an says was there to teach – he left behind the Al-Kitab.*
➤ *What about those who do not understand the Qur'an.*
➤ *It does not cover modern-day problems.*
➤ *It is easier to speak to people than to do research from a book.*
➤ *The role of Imams is to provide guidance.*
➤ *All sources of guidance are useful and support people in different way.*
➤ *Reference to Qur'an 2:151.*

Hints and tips

You need to make sure you give arguments to agree **and** to disagree with the statement – if you give only one point of view, then you cannot get above half marks.

Your answer must be full of religious content – this is a statement about religious beliefs and teachings.

The top level requires good development of the arguments you present. This means giving the argument and explaining clearly why it supports/contradicts the statement using detailed examples. This level is looking for a lot of development.

Try to get into the habit of offering three for and three against arguments in all your AO2 answers. Explain and provide examples for each, and include teachings if possible – this will help push your response to a higher level.

Question 2
Student A

(a) B: Tawalla

(e) **The other three are obligations but not the correct definition.   1 mark**

(b) Purifies money, helps the poor.

(e) **Two correctly identified benefits/positives about Zakah.   2 marks**

(c) Sunnis believe the origins of Ashura were that Muhammad saw the Jews fasting on the tenth Muharram and asked them why. They said because Moses fasted. Muhammad (pbuh) said that they were closer to Musa than the Jews so he told the Muslims to fast.

Shi'a believe the origins go back to the martyrdom of Hussein, the grandson of Muhammad (pbuh), who was killed in battle at Karbala on the tenth Muharram. Hussein was not willing to follow Yazid and had taken his family to Makkah. On the way there they were intercepted and held as captives. The family were attacked and Hussein beheaded.

(e) **This student gives two clearly contrasting views, each with a developed explanation.   4 marks**

(d) Qur'an 96 says to 'Prostrate and draw near to Allah'. Muslims believe a person is closest to Allah when praying and five prayers were instructed by Allah, so whoever does them will be allowed into paradise which is the whole point of this life here and now. Muslims believe that prayer brings knowledge, because by praying sincerely a person's heart is opened to Allah and helps them become more aware of Allah, so more faithful. Muhammad (pbuh) considered anyone not praying five times a day to be unbelievers. People who pray properly will benefit on Judgement Day, and if that prayer is in the mosque Muslims believe the rewards are 27 times greater than praying alone.

(e) **This is an excellent answer stating two ways, clearly showing the importance of prayer and including a relevant quote.   5 marks**

(e) Hajj is the fifth Pillar of Islam and it could be seen as the most important Pillar because it generally only happens once in a lifetime. During the journey you experience things that you can't anywhere else. It brings a Muslim in sight of the Ka'ba – the closest they can be to Allah whilst on earth. Here they say 'here I am Oh lord, here I am' showing that they feel in the presence of Allah. They can walk in the footsteps of famous Muslims like Ibrahim, Adam and Hajara and most importantly they can have their sins forgiven on Mt Arafat and walk away with a renewed sense of Allah being the focal point of their lives. For some though they go with all the best intentions, experience Hajj and then on return soon go back to their old ways so the long lasting effect of Hajj is not there. Salah in comparison reaps great rewards for Muslims and done every day keeps them closer to Allah and stops them going astray so this is far more important. Prayer puts them in Allah's presence everyday not just once.

Other Muslims would say that Shahadah is the most important as without this belief the religion does not exist at all. In other words without this belief in Allah and Muhammad (pbuh) none of the other Pillars would get done at all. Sawm is fasting, which is directed in the Qur'an Surah 2, telling Muslims that they 'gain awareness' from doing so and Zakah Surah 2 also tells them that they should be steadfast in their giving. Both reap great reward.

In conclusion I think we need to think about the diagrams we see of the Pillars; we see that each Pillar is equal in size. The reason for this is so that they are seen as equally important. There are benefits to each one, and simply because one is first, or one is done more regularly than another, this does not lead to one being seen as more important than another. For a Muslim to be true to their faith, all must be done to the best of their ability. There are arguments for each one being more important but this is a misunderstanding of the foundations of the religion. All need to be upheld for the faith to be solid. If they put more emphasis on one than the other then the religion starts to break up.

(e) **This student has structured the answer well, with a diverse range of ideas in each paragraph. Some thoughtful points made and quotes used. Balanced evaluation throughout and an excellent conclusion to bring all the ideas together.   L4: 12 marks**

Question 2
Student B

(a) Nahi Anil-Munkar

(e) **Incorrect. The correct answer is B: Tawalla. This question relies entirely on knowledge of these key words – you need to learn them.   0 marks**

(b) Zakah is one of the five pillars and is given during Ramadan.

(e) **This student clearly does not understand the word 'benefit' as the answer tells us what Zakah is and when it is given.   0 marks**

(c) Shi'a believe Ashura goes back to the martyrdom of Hussein the grandson of Muhammad (pbuh) who was killed in battle at Karbala on the 10th Muhurram. Sunnis believe the origins of Ashura were that Muhammad (pbuh) saw the Jews fasting on the 10th Muharram so he decided to as well.

(e) **This answer states two contrasting views but offers only a simple explanation of each.   2 marks**

(d) Prayer is important to Muslims in two ways. Firstly to pray together in a mosque is a reminder of the greatness of Allah and how much Muslims need him and secondly, it encourages positive qualities such as modesty and humility.

(e) **The responses are too simple; to access the 2 marks available for each, further explanation or examples need to be included. No teaching is included in this answer, so the fifth mark is lost.   2 marks**

(e) Some Muslims would agree with this statement. It is a once in a lifetime experience, walking in the footsteps of their prophets, seeing the Ka'ba, standing on Mt Arafat asking for their sins to be forgiven, rejecting the devil by throwing stones at the pillars at Mina and sacrificing an animal to be given to the poor like Ibrahim did after he passed his test from Allah. Also by being there with other Muslims it gives them a sense of brotherhood and community which actually can only be experienced at Hajj. Most people only get to go once and in poorer countries people who have been are seen as very important within their village, as if they now have greater understanding or awareness than those who have not been.

However others might compare Hajj to Salah and say that this is more important. It is done five times a day and brings people close to Allah. It unites Muslims in the mosque on Fridays and teaches Muslims great qualities like humility, modesty, cleanliness and the acceptance that Allah is far greater than we are. As all of this is done every day it must have a greater impact than Hajj.

However in conclusion others would disagree because it is very difficult to say if any of the Pillars are actually more important. In fact they are all meant to be equal so when they are done and how often they are done is not meant to make one more important than the other.

ℯ **This is a good, clear response. Both sides of the question are argued well with a variety of reasons in them so this is definitely marked at L3. However many of the points could have been developed further; at the moment they read too much like a list. Islamic teaching needs to be included, together with more actual evaluation of the points.   L3: 8 marks**

Mark scheme

2   **(a)** 1 mark for the correct answer.
The correct answer is B: Tawalla

Hints and tips

These questions usually rely entirely on knowledge of key words and terms – you need to learn them. Be careful to read the question carefully as it could ask you what something IS or what it IS NOT.

(b) 1 mark per correct answer, up to 2 marks maximum.
Answers might include:
purifies money, prevents greed, leaves the giver clean, shares the blessings from Allah, 'a hundredfold reward' in the afterlife, helps benefit the Muslim community, helps those in need, feels the joy of giving from the heart

Hints and tips

Do not explain anything unless instructed to – just give two words or phrases to answer this question. That frees up your time to answer later questions.

(c) Total of 4 marks.
For the first view given:
– a **simple** explanation of one view   (1 mark)
– a **detailed** explanation of one view   (2 marks)
For the second view given:
– a **simple** explanation of a contrasting view   (1 mark)
– a **detailed** explanation of a contrasting view   (2 marks)
Answers might include:
Sunni view *– Muhammad was in Madinah and he saw the Jews fasting on the tenth of Muharram. He asked them what they were doing and they explained that it was a day to remember when the Israelites were saved from the Pharaoh. They said that Moses fasted on this day. He replied that 'we are closer to Musa than you'. So he fasted on the day and told the people to fast. There are no Hadith to support this but many Muslims accept its authenticity. Ramadan was established later in Madinah replacing the fast in Muharram.*

Shi'a view – *remembers the martyrdom of Hussein, the grandson of Muhammad, killed in the battle of Karbala on tenth Muharram, along with 72 members of his family. He was killed by Yazid, who had demanded Hussein to give him his allegiance. He refused because of the corruption, first of Maawiyah, then his son, Yazid, who he saw as illegitimate leaders. Hussein had taken his family to Makkah hoping he would be safe. On his way to Kufa in Iraq, he was intercepted and driven into Karbala by 30,000 soldiers. They were held without water. Hussein realised it was him they wanted and told the others to leave, but they refused and were soon attacked. Hussein was beheaded, the camp set fire to and everyone murdered. Bodies were mutilated and left unburied.*

Hints and tips

You have to give two **different** elements when asked for contrast – only writing about one element is worth a maximum of 2 marks.

Try to make sure you are developing your ideas, not just writing lists of new ideas.

(d) Total of 4 marks + 1 mark

Look for explanation of two different ways in the answer.

For the first way given:
- a **simple** explanation of a way which is both clearly relevant to the question and accurate **(1 mark)**
- a **detailed** explanation of a way which is both clearly relevant to the question and accurate **(2 marks)**

For the second way given:
- a **simple** explanation of a way which is both clearly relevant to the question and accurate **(1 mark)**
- a **detailed** explanation of a way which is both clearly relevant to the question and accurate **(2 marks)**

A relevant and accurate reference to scripture and/or sacred writing has been given. **(1 mark)**

Answers might include:

Muslims believe a person is closest to Allah in prayer (Qur'an 96:19) – they were instructed by Allah so whoever does them will be allowed into paradise.

It is believed that prayer brings knowledge, because by praying sincerely a person's heart is opened to Allah and helps them become more aware of Allah and so more faithful.

Prayer with others in the atmosphere of the mosque is a reminder of the greatness of Allah (and the insignificance of humans). It also reminds Muslims that everything comes from and belongs to Allah.

It encourages positive and respectful behaviour, as it is a reminder of good qualities such as modesty, humility, kindness and peace. The process of preparing for prayer is a reminder of cleanliness, purity and determination.

Hints and tips

You have to explain two **different** ways in which Salah is important in the answer to this question.

The mark scheme tells you that the points have to be 'clearly relevant' – if you write something that does not make sense, or that you have to think about to make it relevant, then it is not a good answer.

A good way to answer is to give a way in which Salah is important to Muslims, and then explain it (rather than adding a teaching at the end of the answer).

This is a good example of the importance of knowing key terms – if you do not know this term, or confuse 'Salah' with anything else, then you will lose all the marks.

(e) These questions are marked according to levels of response – this means your answer is judged for its quality overall, not for how many different arguments you present.

Answers might include:

Arguments in support

- *Story of Lazarus at the rich man's gate – we should help those we see*
- *It is not such a massive problem so easier and cheaper to help*
- *If we can't help our own how can we help others?*
- *If we help our own society it makes our society better and safer to live in*
- *Arguments in support of other views*
- *People in other countries have far greater need – they are in abject poverty whereas in the UK they are not*
- *People outside the UK cannot help themselves and the fault of being in poverty is not their own – climate, war, debt etc. whereas fault maybe can be attributed to some of the poor in the UK*
- *The Bible teachings to help all – 'love neighbour', 'what is done for others is done for me'*
- *A small amount goes a long way*
- *Jesus often helped the most needy in society so Christians should follow the example*
- *There are other groups like the government to help in the UK*

Hints and tips

You need to make sure you give arguments to agree **and** to disagree with the statement – if you give only one point of view, then you cannot get above half marks.

Your answer must be full of religious content – this is a statement about religious beliefs and teachings.

The top level requires good development of the arguments you present. This means giving the argument and explaining clearly why it supports/contradicts the statement using detailed examples. This level is looking for a lot of development.

Try to get into the habit of offering three for and three against arguments in all your AO2 answers. Explain and provide examples for each, and include teachings if possible – this will help push your response to a higher level.

Paper 2A Thematic Studies Sample set 1

Theme A: Relationships and families

Question 1

Student A

(a) D: annulment

(e) **Annulment refers to a marriage that has been cancelled, i.e. ended as if it had never happened. This term is used in the Roman Catholic Church.   1 mark**

(b) Nuclear family and extended family.

ⓔ Two types of family correctly identified.   2 marks

(c) Christianity (especially Roman Catholics) teaches that sex is a gift from God for the purpose of procreation and love between a couple and this gift is the gift to a married couple. Sex before marriage is seen as fornication and St Paul in the Bible encourages marriage where passion cannot be controlled.

Islam sees sex before marriage as punishable with 100 lashes under Shari'ah Law as it is seen as zinah which is a sexual offence. It is viewed as casual sex which not only undermines the status of the family with possible unwanted children but also can lead to other acts like rape.

ⓔ This is a good answer as it is not easy to find differences on this topic. Athough they are both saying sex before marriage is wrong the reasons behind the belief and the outcomes are the contrasting issues. Both are clearly stated and have a developed explanation.   4 marks

(d) In Christianity marriage is a sacrament – a commitment made in front of God and the vows in the ceremony tell Christians that it is a lifelong commitment 'till death do us part'. The couple is expected to love and cherish each other, be faithful and to support each other in good and bad times. The Bible says 'It is not good that man should be alone', 'take wives and have sons and daughters' which suggests that marriage is all part of God's plan and the purpose is to be companions to each other and have children.

In Islam according the The Hadith, it is believed that 'there is no institution in Islam more beloved and dearer (to Allah) than marriage', clearly showing that to get married is to please Allah. Marriage should be lifelong, faithful, respectful and fulfil the couple in all ways. There should be respect and kindness shown to each other and to any resulting children.

ⓔ Two distinct teachings are explained clearly. Both paragraphs would be awarded the 2 marks available and the fact that actual specific teachings are referred to would access all 5 marks.   5 marks

(e) The key to this question is that the couple is religious and this for many makes a difference when discussing divorce. A religious couple have married in a church under the eyes of God, have made promises to each other and committed to a lifelong partnership. The marriage has been blessed by God and the couple have promised to be faithful, to look after each other and that 'only death' shall part them. With all this it seems that they should not be allowed to divorce as they were aware of how important it was before they made this commitment. However, things happen in a marriage that cannot be forecasted and maybe the couple has worked at it but something stops them living as a married couple. Perhaps one has been unfaithful and yes they shouldn't do this, but it does happen. How can the other partner ever trust the person again? Or perhaps there is abuse so they cannot stay together as it isn't safe. Just being religious doesn't stop a couple facing difficulties that other couples do. We are all human, make mistakes and hurt other people.

Religion itself would prefer couples not to divorce and some even say it angers God. For Muslims, the Qur'an says 'Paradise shakes at the thought of divorce' which suggests God's anger and that if a man and woman are in danger of splitting then 'two arbiters' should be appointed, the purpose of which is to help sort out the differences. However at the same time, it is said that 'Divorce is the most hated of all the Halal practices' which suggests that while it is hated, it is allowed. There is a process in place to allow it to happen as a last resort. This suggests the statement is wrong. Christianity also has the same idea that Christians should not divorce as God hates it, and that second chances according to the Bible, like remarriage, cause them to commit adultery. Roman Catholics do not actually allow it so whilst by law they can divorce, the church does not recognise that divorce. Other Christian groups though would say that sometimes divorce is the lesser of two evils and sometimes it is necessary though not encouraged.

In conclusion I feel that all religions would actually agree with the statement because no religion advocates divorce and it is the expectation that when a couple marry, they won't divorce as this makes a mockery of their promises. However in reality, they mostly all agree that as a last resort it is acceptable. People, whether religious or not, make mistakes and should not be punished lifelong for that. They may also be the innocent partner in the problems too. Also many religions offer remarriage which recognises this fact. Divorce in a modern world has to be allowed for everyone, but the fact is that this should not mean that the option is abused so that marriage vows become pointless and meaningless.

(e) **Superb! Great evaluation of each point. Many teachings and examples to support each argument and the answer comes to a logical, reasoned conclusion.   L4: 12 marks**

Question 1
Student B

(a) A: divorce

(e) **Incorrect. The correct answer is D: annulment. Make sure you learn the definitions of key words and terms.   0 marks**

(b) Nuclear family where there is just mum, dad and children and single-parent where a child lives with either mum or dad only.

(e) **Two types of family identified but the question does not ask for explanation, so do not waste time giving it.   2 marks**

(c) The rules of the Church of England recognise that in Britain today there is a variety in the situations that people call families. It stresses that marriage is the ideal place for sex, so would not say it is fine, but at the same time they accept that if the sexual relationship is within a permanent, loving relationship, then this is also acceptable.

(e) **This is a developed answer worth the full 2 marks for one belief.   2 marks**

Christianity teaches that sex is a gift of marriage so sex before marriage is not acceptable.

(e) **The second paragraph only really contains a single idea and does not really state which Christian group it refers to, as required by the need to contrast beliefs. If the belief of a different religion is used, the contrast is clearer.   3 marks**

(d) For Muslims marriage is expected of all people and it should be lifelong with no divorce as Allah doesn't like that. It is a gift of God and they should treat each other well because if marriage works out well so does society. In Christianity marriage is becoming less common because people choose to live together.

(e) **The part of the answer on Islam provides just enough explanation to be worth 2 marks – it is a little disjointed but the meaning is there, but the last sentence is just a simple statement which is not enough to gain a mark for 'a simple explanation'. It is also more of a social comment rather than being based on a religious teaching. No quote is used in either part so the fifth mark awarded for 'reference to religious teaching' cannot be gained here.   2 marks**

(e) Divorce is not liked by any religious group really. In marriage ceremonies the two people promise to love each other, take care of each other and be together till death so divorce breaks these promises. These promises for religious people are made in front of God in church for Christians and so Christianity would agree with the statement because people should not break a promise to God. Especially the Roman Catholics think this as they do not allow divorce. Islam even says that divorce makes Allah angry as 'Paradise shakes at the thought of divorce'.

Even though religion doesn't like divorce it seems to accept that there may be a need for it. So whilst they don't like it, as a last resort it may have to happen. For example if a woman is being abused or one of them is an addict, it may be dangerous to stay together especially if there are children in the house. I don't think any religion would seriously disagree with a divorce in these cases. Even Islam allows it in the end after everyone has fought to save the couple.

I believe that even for religious people things happen in life that we don't expect. I think it is true that religious people shouldn't get divorced but in the real world it may be necessary. They obviously married with the intention of keeping the promises but something happened to make it not possible. We should give them a second chance of happiness. I also don't think repeated divorces should be allowed but once it might be needed.

(e) **This answer certainly covers many points on both sides but these points are made superficially. The first section is better quality and supported by teachings. The conclusion makes sense but again touches rather superficially on the issues.   L3: 8 marks**

Mark scheme

1   **(a)** 1 mark for the correct answer.

The correct answer is D: annulment

Hints and tips

These questions usually rely entirely on knowledge of key words and terms – you need to learn them.

Be careful to read the question carefully as it could ask you what something IS or what it IS NOT.

(b) 1 mark per correct answer, up to 2 marks maximum.

Answers might include:

nuclear, extended, single-parent, polygamous.

Hints and tips

Do not explain anything unless instructed to – just give two words or phrases to answer this question. That frees up your time to answer later questions.

The language of questions is really important. For this topic, 'types', 'causes', 'reasons', 'effects' and 'consequences' are all words that could be used by the examiner. Make sure you understand what each term is asking for, as if you mix them up you are throwing easy marks away.

(c) Total of 4 marks.

For the first belief given:
- a **simple** explanation of a relevant and accurate point   **(1 mark)**
- a **detailed** explanation of a relevant and accurate point   **(2 marks)**

For the second contrasting belief given:
- a **simple** explanation of a relevant and accurate point   **(1 mark)**
- a **detailed** explanation of a relevant and accurate point   **(2 marks)**

Answers might include:

__Christian__ teaching generally is that sex should only be experienced within marriage, so sex before marriage is wrong. Sex is a gift from God, for the purpose of procreation, but also as a sign of a couple's loving bond. However, this is a gift to a married couple. Sex before marriage is seen by many Christians as fornication, which is a sin. St Paul said: 'Now to the unmarried and the widows I say: It is good for them to stay unmarried, as I am. But if they cannot control themselves, they should marry, for it is better to marry than to burn with passion.'

The General Synod of the Church of England recognises the variety of family forms today. It stresses that while marriage is the ideal context, sexual relationships must be within permanent, loving relationships (which allows sex before marriage).

__Islam__ teaching is that there should be no sex before marriage – this is fornication. According to Shari'ah Law, it is an offence (zinah – sexual offence) which is punishable by lashes. The basis of Islamic society is a solid family and sex before marriage undermines this ideal. Sex is a gift from Allah and should be treated with a sense of responsibility – casual sex may lead to unwanted children or a child who does not know its father.

Hints and tips

You have to give two different ways in which religious beliefs/teachings influence modern British society in the answer to this question – writing about one way can only get you 2 out of 4 marks.

Always read the whole question including the instructions as this could be vital to prevent a wasted answer.

(d) Total of 4 marks + 1 mark

Look for explanation of two different teachings in the answer.

For the first teaching given:
- a **simple** explanation of a teaching which is both clearly relevant to the question and accurate   **(1 mark)**
- a **detailed** explanation of a teaching which is both clearly relevant to the question and accurate   **(2 marks)**

For the second teaching given:
- a **simple** explanation of a teaching which is both clearly relevant to the question and accurate   **(1 mark)**
- a **detailed** explanation of a teaching which is both clearly relevant to the question and accurate   **(2 marks)**

For relevant and accurate reference to scripture and/or sacred writing as required   **(1 mark)**

Answers might include:

Christianity *– Marriage is a sacrament with promises made in front of God, it is a lifelong commitment till death, 'It is not good that man should be alone', 'take wives and have sons and daughters'. Marriage is symbolic of Christ's relationship with the church. 'Therefore a man shall leave his father and his mother and hold fast to his wife, and they shall become one flesh' showing that marriage involves sexual union of the couple.*

Islam *– Marriage is the union of two families as well as the couple, 'the best amongst you are the ones who treat their wives well','… and we created you in pairs, 'He created for you mates from amongst you that you may live in tranquillity with them and He has put love and mercy between your hearts'. A successful marriage is the basis for the well-being of society as respect and kindness are shown in the home which then should be reflected in society as a whole.*

Hints and tips

You have to explain two **different** teachings in the answer to this question.

The mark scheme tells you that the points have to be 'clearly relevant' – if you write something that does not make sense, or that you have to think about to make it relevant, then it is not a good answer.

A good way to answer is to give a teaching, and then explain how it is important.

You do not have to give exact quotations – it is fine to paraphrase. What you have to do is make it obvious that you are referring to something a person definitely said, and that what you say they said is approximately right. This is especially true when you are referring to a long teaching.

Using key technical terms is always very impressive to the examiner. Try to make sure you use them when you can.

(e) These questions are marked according to levels of response – this means your answer is judged for its quality overall, not for how many different arguments you present.

Answers might include:

Arguments in support of the view:

➤ *Should be a lifelong commitment, not broken promises – Christians make their vows to each other in the church at the altar in front of God.*

➤ *In Christianity marriage is a sacrament – an agreement with God and as marriage symbolises Christ's relationship with the church then it should be lifelong.*

➤ *The Qur'an says that 'God hates divorce', 'paradise shakes at the thought of divorce', 'divorce is the most hated of all halal practices' in Islam.*

➤ *A couple should be prepared to work out their differences especially if children are involved.*

Arguments supporting other views:

➤ *Most religions do not like divorce but accept it including most Christians and all Muslims (divorce is allowable under Shari'ah Law if it is necessary).*

➤ *Just because a couple are religious does not mean they make the right choices if it is.*

➤ *Divorce might be the best possible outcome, e.g. abuse within a marriage.*

➤ *Any couple deserve happiness and a second chance.*

➤ *Divorce is allowed by law.*

➤ *Remarriage is allowed in many Christian churches and in Islam so divorce must be allowed.*

Hints and tips

You need to make sure you give arguments to agree **and** to disagree with the statement – if you give only one point of view, then you cannot get above half marks.

Your answer must be full of religious content – this is a statement about religious beliefs and teachings.

The top level requires good development of the arguments you present. This means giving the argument and explaining clearly why it supports/contradicts the statement using detailed examples. This level is looking for a lot of development.

Try to get into the habit of offering three for and three against arguments in all your AO2 answers. Explain and provide examples for each, and include teachings if possible – this will help push your response to a higher level.

Question 2
Student A

Christianity teaches that there is '… neither male nor female so you are all one in Christ'. This would indicate that as everyone is equal in Christ so they should be equal in society, so gender inequality is wrong as Christians should try to follow the example of the Bible.

Islam teaches '… we created you from a single woman and a single man…' showing that as we all came from the same source there is no reason to treat men and women differently. Also 'everyone is as equal as the teeth on a comb' so again there should be no gender equality issues.

ℯ **This is a good answer, especially as it refers to teachings. Both teachings are clearly stated with a developed explanation linking the teachings to the topic of the question.   4 marks**

Question 2
Student B

The beliefs of the Catholic Church who are Christians are that women cannot be leaders or priests, or lead services, so if a woman wanted to be a priest she couldn't, so this would be gender prejudice. The church though would say that women and men have different roles but are still equal.

Muslims also could be guilty of gender prejudice as only men can be Imams.

ℯ **This answer does not have the clarity of Student A's response and refers to practices rather than beliefs, therefore not showing as much knowledge. The first part is a developed response but the second part is weak.   3 marks**

Mark scheme

2   Total of 4 marks.

For the first belief given:
- ▷ a **simple** explanation of a relevant and accurate point   **(1 mark)**
- ▷ a **detailed** explanation of a relevant and accurate point   **(2 marks)**

For the second similar belief given:
- ▷ a **simple** explanation of a relevant and accurate point   **(1 mark)**
- ▷ a **detailed** explanation of a relevant and accurate point   **(2 marks)**

Answers might include:

__General responses__ – men and women are all creations of God so they should all be able to devote their lives to the service of God; women could in some cases do a better job than a man because of the caring nature of the role; the roles may be different but still equal; gender equality is only an issue if the woman feels she is denied the chance to do something because she is a woman.

__Christianity__ – some of the earliest converts to Christianity were women; Paul states that both men and women are equal in Christ, all are created in the image of God; in the Catholic Church all priests are men but in the Church of England and Non-Conformist churches women can be priests/leaders as in the Early Church the apostles confirmed some women as leaders, e.g. Priscilla.

__Islam__ – all imams are men and women pray behind men; men and women have the same spiritual nature; Prophet Muhammad commanded people to be kind to women. And he said that anyone who does a good deed for Allah will be rewarded (Qur'an 16:97).

Hints and tips

Make sure the similarities you give match-up between the two religious traditions you are referring to.

Question 3

Student A

Most Christian teachings are against divorce and state that marriage is a lifelong commitment until death. Catholic Christians do not accept divorce at all as the vows taken are sacred promises and the marriage is blessed by God. If a divorced person wished to marry again they would not be allowed to in a church service.

In Islam although all Muslims knows that the Qur'an teaches divorce is wrong and that it is a hated practice, they do realise that it might on occasions be necessary. Everything is done to keep the couple together but Shari'ah Law does legislate for it. So it is the most hated of all the halah (allowed) practices.

ⓔ   **A good answer. Both points are clearly stated with a developed explanation linking belief and practices.   4 marks**

Question 3

Student B

For Roman Catholics divorce is always wrong as marriage is a vow that cannot be broken. In other Christian groups divorce is discouraged but it is accepted as a last resort as it is the lesser of two evils of a couple staying together.

ℯ Two points, each with a 'simple' explanation in the last part of each sentence, but no development.   **2 marks**

Mark scheme

3 Total of 4 marks.

For the first belief given:
- ▷ a **simple** explanation of a relevant and accurate point — (1 mark)
- ▷ a **detailed** explanation of a relevant and accurate point — (2 marks)

For the second contrasting belief given:
- ▷ a **simple** explanation of a relevant and accurate point — (1 mark)
- ▷ a **detailed** explanation of a relevant and accurate point — (2 marks)

Answers might include:

General responses *– divorce in most religions is frowned upon and discouraged rather than not being allowed; it is a last resort, the lesser of two evils as it breaks the marriage vows; in a world like today it has to be allowed to protect people; circumstances are considered and reconciliation is recommended.*

Christianity *– vows should not be broken easily; divorce is the lesser of two evils; couples should have a second chance at happiness; divorcees should not be made out to be villains. Roman Catholics do not allow divorce and therefore anyone who had divorced by law would not be able to remarry with a church service. They do allow annulment which is like the marriage never existed, e.g. if it was never consummated. Other Christian churches, whilst they do not agree with divorce realise there might be a necessity for it so can remarry divorced people.*

Islam *– vows should not be broken easily; paradise shakes due to divorce; it is the most hated of all halal practices; efforts should be made to fix marriage; it is easier for a man to divorce than a woman because of society's views; a divorced woman can often end up destitute and unable to remarry even though this is contrary to Qur'anic teaching as it states 'divorced women should have maintenance as this is considered fair; this is the duty of those mindful of God' (2:241).*

Hints and tips

Make sure you do not just state the differences, e.g. in the format '_____ don't allow_____ but _____ do allow ___', as this does not give even a 'simple' explanation.

Theme B: Religion and life

Question 1

Student A

(a)   C: evolution

(e)   **Correct. Charles Darwin developed the theory of natural selection of species in his theory of evolution.   1 mark**

(b)   Reduce greenhouse gases through less pollution and recycle waste so it is not burnt or put it in landfill.

(e)   **Excellent response – the brief explanation for each is not necessary but does provide a clear answer.   2 marks**

(c)   Christians believe in the 'stewardship' that God gave us, to look after animals, so they should disagree with animal experimentation because the animals suffer greatly and even if they do survive the experiment they are disposed of anyway. The Pope said that 'labs of death should be abolished' showing these places cause death. Christians generally though agree with medical experimentation as long as the animals are put through as little suffering as possible, but disagree with experiments for cosmetics because this is unnecessary.

Many Muslims accept experimentation as long as it leads to helping human life, is as a medicine. Life is sacred, so should be protected. Medical advances are an improvement. They would not accept experiments for cosmetics because these are not needed for health, they are just about vanity.

(e)   **This response clearly contrasts the Christian view with the Muslim view and uses a quote. It picks out different Christian views as well as the Muslim view.   4 marks**

(d)   In the Qur'an, Islam teaches 'Neither kill nor destroy yourself'. Obviously euthanasia is where someone agrees to be killed, so is against this teaching. The Qur'an also says that the person who hurries up their own death will be judged badly at Judgement Day – they have no right to decide on their own life because it belongs to Allah.

Christians believe that the Bible says 'Do not kill' and if they put this together with the teaching that God gives life and God takes it away then many Christians would disagree with euthanasia, especially if it is active euthanasia. We cannot act as God would and as he is all-loving he will help the suffering person without us trying to intervene.

(e)   **Two superb explanations. A number of teachings and quotes are used concisely to give the two religious perspectives required.   5 marks**

(e)   In the Bible in God's creation story He makes humans His most intelligent beings and gives them the instruction to be 'stewards' of that creation. This gave mankind the duty to 'look after the world', and as it is God's gift and our existence depends on the environment then it should be our priority. Humanity without the world will die out as we depend on its produce and stability for our long-term survival. In Islam, Muslims are told that 'the world was created as a mosque' and deliberate wrecking of that mosque would be totally unacceptable, so therefore Muslims must look after the world just as much as they would a mosque. Even until Judgement Day they are told that when this happens if they have a 'tree shoot in their hand' they should still plant it. All religious holy books and teachings of key people like the Pope teach people about the world being a priority for this generation and the next and the punishment that will face us if we don't care for the planet. As the role of all people is for eternal life or the ending of the cycle of rebirth then it is in our interest to make the planet a priority in our lives. If we all did the simple things like recycling or using less fuel what a massive difference it would make. Nature might also provide all the answers to cures for human diseases and without nature humanity will face grim deaths whilst nature could help us avoid that suffering.

Whilst it can't be argued that the environment should not be a priority, the issues of living in this world mean that there are plenty of equally important priorities for humans. There are still people starving, when there is excess food and massive waste, and people die through no food or clean water. For a mother who watches her children die, I'm guessing the planet isn't her first priority? However if we had got the planet as our priority years ago then perhaps she would not be in that position now. But this is no answer to her at this point. People face war and terrorism here and now whereas the planet is more of a long-term issue. Humanity and the sacredness of life have always been seen as priority over and above nature. There are people who do make the environment their top priority but they have the means to do this and are now facing other crisis issues.

I don't think that anything in particular needs to be a priority. We all need to find balances in life and work together to solve small and large-scale issues because this can be done if we want it enough. Nature and humanity have to co-exist and if both are looked after then both benefit. If we look after the planet, we have a better environment to live in – more of everything, more beautiful places, and so on – so we benefit. Everything has to be done in equal balance so that nothing is given a priority but each issue is dealt with alongside others.

ⓔ **This is an excellent quality answer. The writing flows and the student uses teachings well, integrating them into the answer rather than simply writing them down in the hope of gaining marks. It is logical and well evaluated with a very good conclusion.   L4: 12 marks**

Question 1
Student B

(a) B: the Genesis creation story

ⓔ **Incorrect. The correct answer is C: evolution. Make sure you learn the key words and terms.   0 marks**

(b) recycle, use less fuel

ⓔ **Very simple, but as correct as Student A's response.   2 marks**

(c) Many Christians agree with the Pope who said that 'labs of death' should be shut. This means that any experiment on an animal is wrong because one way or another they end up dead.

Other Christians would agree with experiments as long as it is to find out about the action of medicines and not for cosmetics like soaps and shampoos. The experiments have to be done as humanely as possible and only if it is 'caring for or saving human life'.

ⓔ **This response does show the contrast between two Christian views but does not make it clear which Christians are referred to. Both quotes are from Roman Catholic sources, but there are different Christian groups that would agree with either side of the debate. There would need to be more explanation of each view for the full marks.   2 marks**

(d) The Bible says 'Do not kill' and euthanasia, whatever the reason for doing it, is killing so Christians would be going against the Ten Commandments. Other Christians might say it is an act of kindness though.

Muslims believe that all life is sacred and should be respected. Euthanasia should never be done because we should be helping life not harming it.

(e) **There are two teachings here – one for each religion and they are simply explained. The last sentence in the first paragraph needs expanding or supporting with evidence and the Muslim one perhaps could use an example to develop it too.   3 marks**

(e) Many people will see this statement as correct because without the environment what will humans be left with? We now know more about the damage we have caused with global warming and climate change and we are suffering the effects so it must be seen as a priority. If the ozone continues to be damaged and the world heats up then it won't be fit in the future to live on. God told us to 'love our neighbour' so we have to think of people in the future as well and why shouldn't they have the world in a good state? God also told people to be stewards. A steward is a person who looks after things to keep them safe and if people don't do as he asked them, they will not have eternal life. So by making the planet a priority others will gain and so will we.

Others would say that although it is a duty it is only one of many. If a person lives in poverty or in a war zone or is ill or dying then these are their priorities because they are immediate problems – they are life or death – whereas the planet seems like a long-term problem which has been going on for years even though the problem is getting worse. I think it is easy to forget about caring for the planet because we just accept it as an issue which is always there but we see it as unsolvable to the individual. We then concentrate on something we can sort out more quickly. God said life is sacred so if a person is dying then saving their life is the priority.

I think caring for the world has to be a priority for some people, for example there are many people working in the conservation and sustainable development industries whose job it is to prioritise the world, but ordinary people have so many different issues to face up to. Also some people don't know what to do because they are not aware of the damage being done.

(e) **This student does give both sides of the argument, but their answer lacks depth in that it comes down to only a few ideas and crucially there is only superficial reference to religion. The answer is certainly in L3 but lacks real supporting evidence and teachings.   L3: 7 marks**

Mark scheme

1   **(a)** 1 mark for the correct answer.

   The correct answer is C: evolution

Hints and tips

These questions usually rely entirely on knowledge of key words and terms – you need to learn them.

Be careful to read the question carefully as it could ask you what something IS or what it IS NOT.

(b) 1 mark per correct answer, up to 2 marks maximum.

Answers might include:

cut pollution, use less fossil fuel, walk more, recycle, cut factory waste, stop farmers using pesticides, reduce landfill, use sustainable energy, conservation projects, use less energy, use wind and solar power more

Hints and tips

Do not explain anything unless instructed to – just give two words or phrases to answer this question. That frees up your time to answer later questions.

The language of questions is really important. For this topic, 'types', 'causes', 'reasons', 'effects' and 'consequences' and in this case 'solutions' are all words that could be used by the examiner. Make sure you understand what each term is asking for, as if you mix them up you are throwing easy marks away.

(c) Total of 4 marks.

For the first belief given:
- a **simple** explanation of a relevant and accurate point **(1 mark)**
- a **detailed** explanation of a relevant and accurate point **(2 mark)**

For the second contrasting belief given:
- a **simple** explanation of a relevant and accurate point **(1 mark)**
- a **detailed** explanation of a relevant and accurate point **(2 marks)**

Answers might include:

Christians – *some think experiments on animals are wrong because God gave us stewardship over animals – the duty to look after them. Patently, experimenting on them and causing them to suffer is not stewardship. Pope John Paul II declared 'We must abandon laboratories and factories of death', showing that laboratories for experimentation are simply places of death. Many Christians believe that testing such products as cosmetics is cruel and unnecessary, bringing suffering to God's wonderful creation, and going against St Francis of Assisi's teaching that, as part of the creation, animals deserve respect and protection, which experimentation seems at odds with.*

Roman Catholic Church – *accepts experiments on animals 'within reasonable limits' and only if it is 'caring for or saving human lives' (Catechism of the Catholic Church).*

Judaism – recognises the duty to improve the welfare and well-being of humanity. This includes improving medical science. Where experiments are for this purpose, they would be acceptable as human life has more value.

Islam – *accepts experimentation if it is for medical advancements. Life is sacred, so needs to be protected. Allah has given humans the intelligence to help each other and develop medicine for this purpose. Medical advancement does not mean cosmetic surgery though.*

Hints and tips

You have to give two **different** religious beliefs/teachings in the answer to this question – writing about one way can only get you 2 out of 4 marks.

Always read the whole question including the instructions as this could be vital to prevent a wasted answer.

(d) Total of 4 marks + 1 mark

Look for explanation of two different teachings in the answer.

For the first teaching given:

– a **simple** explanation of a teaching which is both clearly relevant to the question and accurate **(1 mark)**

– a **detailed** explanation of a teaching which is both clearly relevant to the question and accurate **(2 marks)**

For the second teaching given:

– a **simple** explanation of a teaching which is both clearly relevant to the question and accurate **(1 mark)**

– a **detailed** explanation of a teaching which is both clearly relevant to the question and accurate **(2 marks)**

Relevant and accurate reference to scripture and/or sacred writing as required. **(1 mark)**

Answers might include:

Christianity *– 'Life is sacred', 'I, your God, give life, and I take it away', 'do not kill', there is a reason for everything, 'a time to live and a time to die', euthanasia may be seen as an act of kindness, God granted medical knowledge.*

Islam *– 'No one can die except by Allah's will', euthanasia is Zulm – wrong doing against Allah. Allah plans all life's experience so the suffering must have some purpose. 'Neither kill nor destroy yourself' (Qur'an) – so euthanasia goes against this. Belief that life is sacred means a person should protect not end life.*

Hints and tips

You have to explain two **different** teachings in the answer to this question.

The mark scheme tells you that the points have to be 'clearly relevant' – if you write something that does not make sense, or that you have to think about to make it relevant, then it is not a good answer.

A good way to answer is to give a teaching, and then explain how it is important.

You do not have to give exact quotations – it is fine to paraphrase. What you have to do is make it obvious that you are referring to something a person definitely said, and that what you say they said is approximately right. This is especially true when you are referring to a long teaching.

Using key technical terms is always very impressive to the examiner. Try to make sure you use them when you can.

(e) These questions are marked according to levels of response – this means your answer is judged for its quality overall, not for how many different arguments you present.

Answers might include:

Arguments in support of the view:

➤ *If we don't care for the planet then the current human population will find it hard to survive and future generations may be at great risk if the level of damage continues.*

➤ *God gave humanity its first duty of stewardship.*

➤ *All religions talk about nature being part of God or a reflection of God so it must be looked after.*

➤ *Teachings from holy books and religious leaders all emphasise the need to look after the world.*

➤ *Humanity is quite capable of helping the planet so is there any reason not to do so?*

> *We cannot deny we know about the damage caused by global warming/climate change/deforestation and how it is affecting humans now, so we should want to help ourselves.*

Arguments supporting other views:

> *Caring for the planet is a very long term issue which we cannot see the benefits of right now, whereas other issues can see immediate improvement.*
> *For some people in the world, survival is a key issue before anything else.*
> *Some people are still not aware of the damage being done whereas they are aware of poverty or war.*
> *Much damage is large scale and individuals can have little impact.*
> *The planet will survive for present humanity's lifetime so the issue is more of a priority for people in the future.*
> *Some people do not have environmentally friendly choices available, e.g. sustainable energy.*

Hints and tips

You need to make sure you give arguments to agree **and** to disagree with the statement – if you give only one point of view, then you cannot get above half marks.

Your answer must be full of religious content – this is a statement about religious beliefs and teachings.

The top level requires good development of the arguments you present. This means giving the argument and explaining clearly why it supports/contradicts the statement using detailed examples. This level is looking for a lot of development.

Try to get into the habit of offering three for and three against arguments in all your AO2 answers. Explain and provide examples for each, and include teachings if possible – this will help push your response to a higher level.

Question 2

Student A

Christians in Genesis are created as stewards of the world. They were the last of creation and were given the responsibility to look after the world God had created for them. They should look to protect the environment in their own lives and support world environmental protection issues so that God's world can be returned to him at the end of time.

Muslims believe that in the beginning Allah created them as khalifahs of the world and so they have a duty to look after it. Therefore they would support conservation projects so that Allah's world is green and beautiful and they are rewarded for fulfilling their duty.

ⓔ **A good answer – both these points develop the explanation to show why these two religions should look after the world.   4 marks**

Question 2

Student B

Christians believe that God created them as stewards and as such they have a God-given duty to not damage the environment. If they do damage the world then God will punish them in the life to come as 'Everything is the Lord's' and no one wants their designs damaged. Humans on Earth know the damage they do so cannot use ignorance as an excuse.

Muslims have similar teachings about looking after the world and worshipping Allah.

(e) **The first part of this answer is good as it contains teachings and explanations in the context of the question. Always try and use the language of the question, e.g. here use environment not world – it looks better and directly refers to the question itself. The second part, although correct, is too vague – the examiner would have to do too much work to make sense of it and apply it to the question.   2 marks**

Mark scheme

2   Total of 4 marks.

For the first belief given:
- a **simple** explanation of a relevant and accurate point   (1 mark)
- a **detailed** explanation of a relevant and accurate point   (2 marks)

For the second similar belief given:
- a **simple** explanation of a relevant and accurate point   (1 mark)
- a **detailed** explanation of a relevant and accurate point   (2 marks)

Answers might include:

General responses – *reference to the creation and that as God created the world, religious believers should look after it and that there will be rewards for such actions. Individual believers have a responsibility to others to look after the world they live in and preserve it for future generations.*

Christianity – *the world is a gift from God and as such His creation should want to look after it; stewardship is a key duty for all Christians as it was an instruction from God Himself; respect for life; punishment would result from the destruction of nature; everything in the world is the Lord's. 'God looked down on His creation and said that it was good' (Genesis) suggests that humans need to maintain the goodness of the creation; all the damage they do should through pollution etc. should be avoided or put right through conservation and sustainable energies.*

Islam – *the world is green and beautiful; the duty of being khalifahs, or trustees of the world; the Earth is like a place of worship; creation reflects Allah; punishment will follow on the day of judgement; Muslims have a duty to each other to keep the environment viable now and for the future as this is part of the concept of ummah.*

Hints and tips

On a similarities question make sure your two points are written out fully. Your answer cannot simply say that the second religion believes the same as the first without an explanation.

Question 3

Student A

In the Church of England abortion, although not liked, is seen as a necessary evil – for example, where the mother's life is at risk if the pregnancy was to continue. All life is sacred but hers is as well, especially if the woman already has children dependent on her.

The Roman Catholic Church believes that abortion is always murder and that there are other options to abortion like adoption. The unborn child cannot defend itself so it must be protected. All life is in the hands of God and as He determines life and death, the situation should be left in His hands.

ⓔ A good answer – both points show a clear difference of the views within the Christian tradition and develop the explanation.   4 marks

Question 3

Student B

Muslims say that all life is created by Allah and He has a plan for all life and so humans should not be able to decide about abortion.

Other Muslims would say that the soul is not in the body until after 40 or 120 days so to carry out an abortion then is not murder and is allowed.

ⓔ Each part of this response is a simple answer that would need further development to get the 2 marks available for each point.   2 marks

Mark scheme

3   Total of 4 marks.

For the first belief given:
> a **simple** explanation of a relevant and accurate point (1 mark)
> a **detailed** explanation of a relevant and accurate point (2 marks)

For the second contrasting belief given:
> a **simple** explanation of a relevant and accurate point (1 mark)
> a **detailed** explanation of a relevant and accurate point (2 marks)

Answers might include:

__General responses__ – life is sacred; it is wrong to kill; abortion is unfair on an innocent foetus; life needs to be protected; it is not only the foetus that needs to be considered, abortion may be the kindest choice to make and can show compassion.

__Christianity__ – abortion can be considered murder; all life is sacred; it must be considered responsibly; there are reasons where it could be acceptable but at the same time the life of the unborn needs protecting; there are other options to abortion like adoption. The Bible says 'Do not kill' and 'He knew you before you were born' showing the value of life and suggests that even before birth an individual soul is known to God. Roman Catholics say abortion can never be justified and that life must be protected from conception to natural death. The rights of the unborn child exceed the life of the mother. Other Christian groups agree abortion is wrong but maybe a necessary evil in some situations.

Islam – *abortion is against Allah's plan; Allah takes life; ensoulment happens at 40 or 120 days so if there is no soul then abortion is allowed – here showing before 40 days for some it is acceptable or before 120 days for others it is acceptable as life begins when the soul is 'breathed by Allah'; a woman's life at risk would see Muslims support abortion as she already has responsibilities and may have other children. The Qur'an says 'each person is created from a single clot of blood' by Allah and as such all life is intentional on His part, so to destroy would be to destroy His creation. The soul of an aborted child can question its mother on Judgement Day.*

Hints and tips

Be sure to develop each point you make. Use examples or further explanation to pick up the second mark available on each point.

Theme C: The existence of God and revelation

Question 1

Student A

(a) C: someone who isn't sure if God exists or not

e **Correct. An agnostic does not accept that there is enough evidence to persuade them either way in determining God's existence.   1 mark**

(b) They are insane and so hallucinated or they were ill and so hallucinated.

e **Two clear ideas provided.   2 marks**

(c) Some religious people like Christians think miracles are actions of God. God is all-loving and all-powerful, so when someone needs help from God, God helps them. For example, a person might be very ill, so that doctors say they will die as they cannot be cured. Everyone prays for them to recover and they do. They then believe that God performed a miracle.

An atheist would say that the word miracle is just a word we use when we can't explain something. In the example of a dying person who is suddenly better, the atheist would say this was just a part of nature and medicine that we don't yet understand and can't explain. There is no such thing as God so there is no God to perform a miracle.

e **Two clear, detailed explanations for 'miracles' which are clearly differing views.   4 marks**

(d) Christians believe that God speaks directly to human beings in special revelation. For example, in the Bible it says Saul was blinded in a revelation when Jesus said 'why do you persecute me?' After this revelation he called himself Paul and became a Christian. God had a task for Saul so Jesus gave him that task in the revelation. God uses revelations to get messages to humans.

They also believe that God spoke to Moses from a burning bush. Moses could see the bush was in flames but not actually being damaged. God's voice came from it and told him that he was to save the Israelites from slavery in Egypt.

e **Two explanations given clearly and in detail – in other words, a developed answer. There is reference to scripture as required.   5 marks**

(e) I think some people might agree with that statement. Many scientists are not religious; they look for rational explanations for things, for fact to prove their theories. Religion relies on belief in unprovable ideas – no proof is needed. These are opposites and not compatible. Also, when you look at their beliefs about the origins of the universe there are many incompatibilities. Science says this happened billions of years ago; fundamental Christians say God created the world just 6,000 years ago. Science describes an accidental explosion; religion says there was a deliberate and designed creation. Science says that what we see now evolved over millions of years; religion says God created the world and all life. Even if the Bible doesn't say exactly what God made, i.e. naming species, it does say he made fish and birds – which are far down the evolution chain. So the two descriptions of the origins are totally different, and that makes them incompatible. The most fundamental thing though is that religion says God did it, whereas science explains everything without God. Scientists do not look for God in a story, they write God out of them – including stories about the origins of the universe.

However, I also think that people can believe in both science and religion, and can see them as compatible. Indeed people do! Rev Sir T Polkinghorne was a Professor of Science at university – the fact he is also a reverend proves he can do science and religion. In terms of origins of the universe, religious people might say religious stories tell us why it all happened, and science tells us how – this means that they simply address different questions so can't clash. They are compatible. Others may say that God created the world by means of what science says – God made the Big Bang happen and set off evolution. Again this means there is no incompatibility. Finally we have to remember that when Genesis was written, people had a limited understanding of science – they created a reasonable explanation of how the world began. When compared to science, Genesis starts with light (explosion) and the world's development and development of life is similar to how science says it happened – it is just a simple version compared to the complex science one.

ⓔ **Two sides of the argument are clearly explained in this answer. As a matter of writing style, it is always good to use 'some' and 'others' rather than 'I think' and then 'I also think'. This is because in an evaluation you are often looking at opposite ideas and to think two opposite things at the same time is not really possible. The student has not given a conclusion.   L4: 10 marks**

Question 1
Student B

(a) A: someone who doesn't believe God exists

ⓔ **Incorrect. The correct answer is C: someone who isn't sure if God exists or not. Make sure you learn these key words.   0 marks**

(b) They are insane so they see things that aren't there, so are hallucinating.

ⓔ **This answer gives one, not two, ideas and even though it is explained it is still only one idea.   1 mark**

(c) Miracles are impossible events which break down the laws of nature. A religious person would think they happened because God made them happen. A humanist doesn't believe in God. They would look for another explanation, so they might say that the person who claimed something to be a miracle was biased. They expect good things to happen because God does miracles, so they label things miracles when they aren't.

(e) **This student gives two clear, different ideas but does not explain them, specifically refer to a religion or give examples. 2 marks**

(d) Muslims believe that Allah's teachings were revealed to Prophet Muhammad by Angel Jibr'il on Mt Hira. These revelations made up the Qur'an when written down.

(e) **This answer has no scripture reference and both ideas need further development in order to gain full marks. 2 marks**

(e) On the one hand, some would agree with the statement because many scientists don't believe in God so he cannot have started the universe. Religious people who believe in God accept the Genesis creation story with God starting it all off. Also science wants answers to things that can be proved by evidence or testing but religion is only about belief so belief doesn't need proving. So with the origins of the universe scientists would say there is evidence for the Big Bang but there is no evidence for God. Science would say that the world is far older than 6,000 years as the Bible suggests so God is not the answer. All this shows that science and religious ideas are incompatible because they are often providing totally opposite ideas.

On the other hand, others would disagree with the statement because science can say the world began with the Big Bang and then life evolved, but religion could say that God caused the Big Bang and then evolution was part of the design. It might also be that the story in Genesis is talking not about days as it has been translated into English but more as periods of time. What is 6 days was actually 6 periods of time with each period being a billion years. In this way science and religion can agree with each other. There are also many scientists who are religious so the two have to be compatible.

I think that science and religion are compatible because science can tell us how, but not always why, whereas religion tells us why, but not always how. If we put the two together, science explains how the universe began and religion explains why it all happened so we then get the full picture.

(e) **This is a good answer which is logically but simply written. It contains lots of ideas which, although simple, make sense and flow well. The conclusion is also reasoned. The weakness is that it reads more like an AO1 response than an AO2 one: evaluation of the ideas is missing. L3: 7 marks**

Mark scheme

1 (a) 1 mark for the correct answer.

The correct answer is C: someone who isn't sure if God exists or not

Hints and tips

These questions usually rely entirely on knowledge of key words and terms – you need to learn them.

Be careful to read the question carefully as it could ask you what something IS or what it IS NOT.

(b) 1 mark per correct answer, up to 2 marks maximum.

Answers might include:

hallucination, under the influence of drugs or alcohol, illness affecting the mind, insanity, misinterpreting any experience, religious bias, desire to see something which leads to 'seeing'

Hints and tips

Do not explain anything unless instructed to – just give two words or phrases to answer this question. That frees up your time to answer later questions.

The language of questions is really important. For this topic, 'types', 'causes', 'reasons', 'effects', 'consequences' and in this case 'explanation' are all words that could be used by the examiner. Make sure you understand what each term is asking for, as if you mix them up you are throwing easy marks away.

(c) Total of 4 marks.

For the first belief given:
- a **simple** explanation of a relevant and accurate point   (1 mark)
- a **detailed** explanation of a relevant and accurate point   (2 marks)

For the second contrasting belief given:
- a **simple** explanation of a relevant and accurate point   (1 mark)
- a **detailed** explanation of a relevant and accurate point   (2 marks)

Answers might include:

Miracles are breaches in the laws of nature which bring good outcomes; attributed to God (all-powerful and all-loving) as God intervenes into our world to make these good and impossible events happen; miracles happen because of the prayers of the faithful, and the intervention/intercession of holy figures, e.g. Mary.

*An **atheist** would dispute that God performs miracles, as, to them, God does not exist. They might see for example a 'miracle recovery' as something which can occur naturally – spontaneous regression – an event which is not yet understood by medical science, but will be at some point in the future.*

*A **humanist** would look to a non-supernatural answer for the event. They can show that events previously classed as miracles are now explicable by medical science, and that those calling them miracles already had a religious bias to affect their interpretation of what they saw.*

Hints and tips

You have to give two **different** beliefs in the answer to this question – writing about one can only get you 2 out of 4 marks. Always read the whole question including the instructions as this could be vital to prevent a wasted answer.

(d) Total of 4 marks + 1 mark

Look for explanation of two different teachings in the answer.

For the first teaching given:
- a **simple** explanation of a teaching which is both clearly relevant to the question and accurate   (1 mark)
- a **detailed** explanation of a teaching which is both clearly relevant to the question and accurate   (2 marks)

For the second teaching given:
- a **simple** explanation of a teaching which is both clearly relevant to the question and accurate   (1 mark)
- a **detailed** explanation of a teaching which is both clearly relevant to the question and accurate   (2 marks)

Relevant and accurate reference to scripture and/or sacred writing as required.   (1 mark)

Answers might include:

- *God speaks **directly to humans** in special revelation – e.g. Saul in the Bible, Prophet Muhammad in the Qur'an.*
- *Some holy books like the Qur'an prove there is special revelation – they exist only because of special revelation, Qur'an 96:1-4. The Ten Commandments were given through special revelation (Exodus 20:1-20).*
- *God **gives instructions and orders to humans** through special revelation, e.g. Qur'an 96:1-4 where Muhammad was instructed to write by Angel Jibrail.*
- *In **Christianity and in Islam** there are examples of special revelation – all include a person gaining **greater understanding of religious truths** through the revelation, so the point of them is to give insight. In the Old Testament, God gives Moses the Ten Commandments, hence showing God is the Law-Giver and that there are basic 'essential' laws; in the Qur'an Muhammad is told what Allah wants from humans, so is able to dictate the Hadith/Sunnah to make others understand what he has realised for himself.*
- *Special revelations are seen to **change lives**, as they influence the attitude of the receiver and make them adopt a new way of seeing and behaving, for example Saul changed from being a hunter of Christians to a great proponent of the faith.*
- *Those who receive special revelations are seen to be blessed – **chosen ones** – with a special authority because of their revelation, e.g. Prophet Muhammad – the Qur'an claims him as the best example for a Muslim to follow.*

Hints and tips

You have to explain two **different** teachings in the answer to this question.

The mark scheme tells you that the points have to be 'clearly relevant' – if you write something that does not make sense, or that you have to think about to make it relevant, then it is not a good answer.

A good way to answer is to give a teaching, and then explain how it is important.

You do not have to give exact quotations – it is fine to paraphrase. What you have to do is make it obvious that you are referring to something a person definitely said, and that what you say they said is approximately right. This is especially true when you are referring to a long teaching.

Using key technical terms is always very impressive to the examiner. Try to make sure you use them when you can.

(e) These questions are marked according to levels of response – this means your answer is judged for its quality overall, not for how many different arguments you present.

Answers might include:

Arguments in support of the view:

➤ *Scientists are not religious.*
➤ *Science looks for facts and rational thinking whereas religion relies on belief with no proof.*
➤ *Belief and rational thinking are opposites.*
➤ *Science says origins were billions of years ago; religion 6,000 years ago.*
➤ *Science says origins are accidental; religion says planned and designed.*
➤ *Science talks of evolution over time whereas religion says God made actual species.*
➤ *Science has no concept of God whereas religion says God created it at the start.*

Arguments supporting other views:

- ➤ *People can believe in both science and religion.*
- ➤ *There are scientist who are religious.*
- ➤ *Science gives the how and religion gives the why; put the two together and we get the full picture so they are compatible.*
- ➤ *God created the world by means of what science says – God made the Big Bang happen and set off evolution.*
- ➤ *Religion gives a reasonable explanation considering the level of scientific knowledge at the time.*
- ➤ *What if the 6 creation 'days' of Genesis was more like 6 periods of time, e.g. 6 billion years – the Hebrew word can be translated as this rather than 'days'.*

Hints and tips

You need to make sure you give arguments to agree **and** to disagree with the statement – if you give only one point of view, then you cannot get above half marks.

Your answer must be full of religious content – this is a statement about religious beliefs and teachings. It will be difficult not to write about religion in the religion-based ones though!

The top level requires good development of the arguments you present. This means give the argument and explain clearly why it supports/contradicts the statement. Using examples helps to further develop your answer – this level is looking for a lot of development, not just very short explanations.

Question 2
Student A

Some religious believers think that God exists through revelation. God reveals Himself so that humans can know something about Him. One way is through special revelation where God directly contacts humans individually or as a group through visions or dreams or through His voice while praying.

Other religious people believe God exists through general revelation. He can use nature, people or events. Holy books are a good example like the Qur'an as the word of Allah. The books are all about God so people learn what God is like from them.

e **A good answer as both points are clearly stated and they both argue that God exists, just through different methods. Each idea develops an explanation.** **4 marks**

Question 2
Student B

Revelation tells some people God exists, like when He speaks to them in their prayers. For others, like Muslims, He must exist because of their Holy Book, the Qur'an which came from Allah though his angel.

e **The two points in this answer gain 1 mark each. They are both a 'simple' explanation of how revelation shows that God exists. To gain the second mark for each point, more detail is needed to make it clearer to the reader.** **2 marks**

Mark scheme

2 Total of 4 marks.

For the first belief given:
- ▷ a **simple** explanation of a relevant and accurate point (1 mark)
- ▷ a **detailed** explanation of a relevant and accurate point (2 marks)

For the second similar belief given:
- ▷ a **simple** explanation of a relevant and accurate point (1 mark)
- ▷ a **detailed** explanation of a relevant and accurate point (2 marks)

Answers might include:

Revelation for some people is a way of confirming the existence of God for that individual. Revelation can be special where contact is made directly from God through dreams, visions or actually hearing His voice.

General revelation is more indirect, for example through something like nature which reveals the beauty and creativity of God, or through holy books which have been revealed though His angels or through His inspiration. These books let humanity know the nature of God in what He wants to reveal to them.

Hints and tips

Your answer would have been exactly the same if the question asked for two different religious beliefs about revelation – one through special revelation and one through general revelation. This will be the case in many of these types of questions so think about this in your revision.

Question 3
Student A

Many Christians believe God is always willing to have a personal relationship because He loves us. This means they can learn about Him and He allows them to learn. Teresa of Avila meditated and wrote a book about her knowledge of God from that meditation, from His grace to let her learn.

Muslims believe in Tawhid, that there is only one God – Allah who is eternal, has no partners, is not born and does not die. This means they cannot really know Allah at all – Allah is too special and different to us. So really, they cannot be enlightened about God. Even if they can know what Allah wants them to do, they can't know about Allah Himself.

ⓔ A good answer as both points are clearly stated and have a developed explanation. **4 marks**

Question 3
Student B

Some religious believers think by reading the holy book they learn about God so get enlightened.

Some religious believers think God is transcendent so they can't become enlightened about him at all.

ⓔ For each point, the minimal necessary is given to achieve a mark. Each point gives a quality of God with a 'simple' explanation in the last part of each sentence. **2 marks**

Mark scheme

3   Total of 4 marks.

For the first belief given:
> a **simple** explanation of a relevant and accurate point   (1 mark)
> a **detailed** explanation of a relevant and accurate point   (2 marks)

For the second contrasting belief given:
> a **simple** explanation of a relevant and accurate point   (1 mark)
> a **detailed** explanation of a relevant and accurate point   (2 marks)

Answers might include:

*Enlightenment is to help you understand yourself, not God, so gives you no knowledge of the divine –
Jesus said 'Physician, heal yourself'; God is transcendent and impersonal, so nothing can give humans
true knowledge of God, even enlightenment; Islam tells us to just believe and accept, as we cannot even
look at God, so how can we know God in any way?*

*Enlightenment is the realisation or full understanding of a religious truth, like that which Teresa
of Avila reached through meditation – she then wrote a book about knowing God; Prophet
Muhammad could tell people what God wanted because of the revelations which gave him a form
of enlightenment; by being enlightened about God, people can relate to God, and/or can describe
aspects of God*

Hints and tips

Make sure that the explanation you give explains the point being made and is not a separate point
altogether.

Theme D: Religion, peace and conflict

Question 1
Student A

(a)   B: making up between two groups who have had a disagreement.

🄔   **Correct. Reconcile means 'to bring together' – a peaceful action so the answer can
only be B.   1 mark**

(b)   Taking or retaking land, self-defence.

🄔   **Two correct ideas.   2 marks**

(c)   The Catholic Church does not accept the use of nuclear weapons in war but does accept their
existence as a deterrent to war. If two countries have them then it can keep the peace between the two
like India/Pakistan for example. Pope John Paul II said this about the weapons: 'in current conditions,
"deterrence" based on balance, certainly not as an end in itself but as a step along the way towards a
progressive disarmament, may still be judged morally acceptable'. If a country is better protected then
they serve a purpose.

Muslims believe from the Qur'an 'Do not contribute to your own destruction with your own hands, but do good deeds, as God loves those who do good', clearly indicating that to use weapons of mass destruction is wrong. However, in practice they in the form of chemical weapons have been used by Muslim governments like Syria and Iraq recently which shows that they not only possess them as a deterrent but are willing to use them even though it goes against their religious teachings.

(e) **In this answer the two beliefs are clearly developed and show a contrasting view on the topic with their approach being slightly different. The fact that the Pope would never sanction their use but some Muslim governments have, despite teachings, shows a clear contrasting view of the willingness to break them or keep them. Excellent answer.   4 marks**

(d) Jesus said 'blessed are the peace makers' in the Beatitudes which seems to suggest that those who promote or work for peace will be rewarded, presumably in Paradise, and this is supported when he says 'those who live by the sword die by the sword' which suggests that those who take up arms ought not to be surprised by dying as a result of use of the same weapons. This teaching emphasises the pointlessness of war and everyone eventually loses out by it.

Muslims believe in peace – in fact the word Islam itself means peace. Muhammad (pbuh) taught 'hate your enemy mildly, for he may become your friend one day' (Hadith) clearly showing that peace is far more important than hate and violence. 'If peace is offered in any situation it should be taken – 'but if they (non-believers) incline towards peace, you must also incline towards it, and put your trust in God.' shows that war should never be continued by Muslims if the other side wants peace as peace overrides everything.

(e) **Excellent answer for both teachings chosen. These attitudes to peace are clearly explained.   5 marks**

(e) This is an issue that has been debated many times throughout history. There is no doubt that some would disagree because religion has been a central issue in many wars both a long time ago and recently. However, just because two sides who are fighting happen to be different religions it does not mean that religion is the actual cause.

The Gulf Wars, Muslims claimed, were an attack on Islam. Israel and Palestine is said to be a Jewish against Muslim conflict and even the acts of terrorists (like in Ireland where recent conflict has been seen as a Catholic and Protestant one) suggest that religion is the cause of war. In contrast though, if we look at religious teachings most of them suggest that wars should not be fought and so for religion to be an actual cause of war would be very strange. Christians are told 'Do not kill' and for 'those who live by the sword, they will die by the sword' so this would dissuade Christians from taking up arms.

Religious teachings do justify war if the religion is under attack but that has never been the case even though some have claimed it. Some people have used religion to gather support for their actions and to drag in others for their cause but actually this isn't really about religion – it is more likely about power and land which religion then gets caught up in.

In many wars religious sites and holy buildings have been seen as unacceptable targets, so if religion was the cause then surely these places would have been hit. If the Gulf War was about religion and an attack on Islam, why invade Iraq when somewhere like Makkah for instance could be bombed, especially as Saudi Arabia borders Iraq and also has oil into the bargain? Likewise in Ireland, why not bomb the many church buildings instead of pubs, for example. All this would suggest religion is a side issue not a cause.

The crusades were possibly the nearest war where religion was a cause, considering that the fight between Christians and Muslims was over the Holy City of Jerusalem to establish it as the centre of belief in either a Christian or Muslim God. Also in many wars it doesn't take long for religions to come to the surface as a conflict issue so some might argue that maybe it is actually a root cause.

Some people might say that religion is not a cause as only a small percentage of that specific group are in favour of the war whereas the majority are against the actions. Many Catholics and Protestants in Ireland, Muslims and Jews in Israel, and Muslims living in Syria, want peace and condemn the violence of those who claim to be members of their religion, so religion is not a cause. Religion has in fact been a key part in ending war, through negotiation, working together, promoting peace and this is far more supported by evidence than religion as a cause of war is.

In conclusion I do not believe religion is the cause of war. It might be used by extremists as an excuse for war but there are too many teachings that the majority of these groups follow to work for peaceful solutions rather than to cause wars.

(e) **This student shows plenty of understanding of the issue and evaluates each idea throughout. Points are supported with examples and teachings that form a comprehensive argument; the conclusion is rational and logical from the evidence evaluated in the answer.** **L4: 12 marks**

Question 1
Student B

(a) A: to take revenge after being invaded or attacked.

(e) **Incorrect. The correct answer is B, making up between two groups who have had a disagreement. Make sure you understand these key words.** **0 marks**

(b) Religion and money.

(e) **Neither of these answers is really specific enough. Religion is debatable – it is involved in acts of war but may not be the actual cause. You might get the mark or you might not, so go for absolute, definite ideas.** **1 mark**

(c) Quakers are pacifists so they believe in the biblical idea of 'do not kill'. This is not dependent upon the situation but all the time. They are weapons that cannot be controlled and kill human life and contaminate areas for many years to come. The world is God's creation and life is sacred so use of WMD can never be supported.

Roman Catholics have a slightly different view. They don't agree with their use but they say a country might be able to protect itself better if they have WMD, especially if it is a small country.

(e) **The first idea is fine, as the student gives a teaching and uses this to explain the Quaker view. The second idea would need more development, with the use of a teaching or supported evidence, to be awarded full marks.** **3 marks**

(d) Christians believe that they should 'love their neighbour' as Jesus told them, so if we do this then we should want to live in peace and not start wars because war is about hate not love.

Muslims believe in peace as peace is what the Qur'an teaches them as there are far greater rewards for peaceful and good actions than bad deeds.

(e) The teachings used in this answer are generic rather than being war/peace specific. They are just as valid but not as impressive at showing knowledge. The first paragraph is quite simple in terms of explanation – it would need further detail/examples to be developed. The same applies to the second paragraph. The teachings are there and so gain the 1 mark awarded for use of teachings.   **3 marks**

(e) I agree that religion is not a cause of war because most wars are fought so leaders can take over another country or to increase their power or reputation. Also some wars are for self-defence or to protect another country from attack. Obviously any war, because it's about different people coming into conflict, might well involve religion, as religion is one of the things humans disagree about, but this does not mean it is the actual thing that started the war. Also religious teachings try to make people live in peace not war so why would people want to use religion to start wars? Many wars are started by political leaders for political gain so religion does not come into it at this point. It might do later but then it is not the first thing which started the war, it is just caught up in it really.

Others might disagree with me and say actually religion does cause wars. It is the thing we have argued about for centuries and in fact there is a lot of hatred between religious groups. This is not only true of one religion against another but also groups against each other within a religion. For example much of the killing by ISLE involves Sunni Muslims killing Shi'a Muslims and in Ireland Catholics killing Protestants. So if religion is not the issue why are they killing each other?

From the two religions I have looked at in my course both say that killing is wrong but they have been involved in wars too over history. Some wars are said to have been holy wars, so religion has to be at the centre of these I think. However, most wars are very complex and not really about one issue and I think that religion might be one of those issues rather than being a main cause.

(e) This student's answer does not flow as well as Student A's response, but there are a number of valid points made and evaluation is attempted. The use of more teachings as a source to support some of the points is needed to make it a better answer. Note that you should never begin an evaluation with 'I agree/disagree…'. Do the evaluation first and then put your view in the conclusion so that the examiner can see how you have weighed up the arguments to reason out your opinion.   **L3: 7 marks**

Mark scheme

1   **(a)** 1 mark for the correct answer.

The correct answer is B: making up between two groups who have had a disagreement.

Hints and tips

These questions usually rely entirely on knowledge of key words and terms – you need to learn them.

Be careful to read the question carefully as it could ask you what something IS or what it IS NOT.

(b) 1 mark per correct answer, up to 2 marks maximum.

Answers might include:

to gain more power, land or resources (greed), for self-defence or to defend others, to protect the rights of people

Hints and tips

Do not explain anything unless instructed to – just give two words or phrases to answer this question. That frees up your time to answer later questions.

The language of questions is really important. For this topic, 'types', 'causes', 'reasons', 'effects' and 'consequences' are all words that could be used by the examiner. Make sure you understand what each term is asking for, as if you mix them up you are throwing easy marks away.

(c) Total of 4 marks.

For the first belief given:
- a **simple** explanation of a relevant and accurate point (1 mark)
- a **detailed** explanation of a relevant and accurate point (2 marks)

For the second contrasting belief given:
- a **simple** explanation of a relevant and accurate point (1 mark)
- a **detailed** explanation of a relevant and accurate point (2 marks)

Answers might include:

*The **Roman Catholic Church** does not agree with the use of weapons of mass destruction. However, it considers them to be currently necessary as a deterrent. 'In current conditions, **"deterrence" based on balance**, certainly not as an end in itself but as a **step along the way towards a progressive disarmament**, may still be judged morally acceptable' (Pope John Paul II). This is because by having these weapons, a country may be better protected against attack by others. The weapons are seen to afford safety and peace. There should be no intention to use them against large populations (indiscriminate killing), and there should be no proliferation (having the biggest quantity). They consider that the only legitimate purpose for nuclear weapons is to prevent war – so they should never need to be used.*

*The **Quaker Society** utterly condemn weapons of mass destruction. They are pacifists, and no outward weapons are acceptable. WMD are indiscriminate and beyond control and so take life – military and non-military – on a massive scale, and destroy even the creation.*

*Some **Muslims** believe that WMD are acceptable to have as they keep the peace – one powerful country will not use these weapons on other countries that possess them too. Only Pakistan as a Muslim country currently possesses a nuclear deterrent (about 120 weapons) and as these may be the reason there is peace with India then there is little campaigning to disarm them. Generally any destruction of life within Islamic belief is wrong – 'Do not contribute to your own destruction with your own hands, but do good deeds, as God loves those who do good'. However, some Muslim countries like Syria and Iraq have used WMD in the form of chemical weapons on their people even though this goes against Muslim teachings.*

Hints and tips

You have to give two **different** beliefs – writing about one can only get you 2 out of 4 marks.

Always read the whole question including the instructions as this could be vital to prevent a wasted answer.

(d) Total of 4 marks + 1 mark

Look for explanation of two different teachings in the answer.

For the first teaching given:

– a **simple** explanation of a teaching which is both clearly relevant to the question and accurate **(1 mark)**

– a **detailed** explanation of a teaching which is both clearly relevant to the question and accurate **(2 marks)**

For the second teaching given:

– a **simple** explanation of a teaching which is both clearly relevant to the question and accurate **(1 mark)**

– a **detailed** explanation of a teaching which is both clearly relevant to the question and accurate **(2 marks)**

Relevant and accurate reference to scripture and/or sacred writing as required. **(1 mark)**

Answers might include:

Christianity – *Put away your sword, 'those who live by the sword die by the sword' (Jesus), 'Blessed are the peacemakers' (Jesus), 'Love your enemies, and pray for them' (Jesus), 'Peace I leave with you, my peace I give to you' (Jesus), 'Everyone must commit themselves to peace' (Pope John Paul II).*

Islam – *greet others salaam alaikum, which means 'peace be upon you', 'hate your enemy mildly, for he may become your friend one day' (Hadith), if peace is offered in any situation it should be taken 'but if they (non-believers) incline towards peace, you must also incline towards it, and put your trust in God..' Qur'an 49:9*

Hints and tips

You have to explain two **different** teachings in the answer to this question.

The mark scheme tells you that the points have to be 'clearly relevant' – if you write something that does not make sense, or that you have to think about to make it relevant, then it is not a good answer.

A good way to answer is to give a teaching, and then explain how it is important.

You do not have to give exact quotations – it is fine to paraphrase. What you have to do is make it obvious that you are referring to something a person definitely said, and that what you say they said is approximately right. This is especially true when you are referring to a long teaching.

Try and learn specific teachings as they serve your argument much better and show greater knowledge than using generic ones everywhere.

(e) These questions are marked according to levels of response – this means your answer is judged for its quality overall, not for how many different arguments you present.

Answers might include:

Arguments in support of the view:

➤ *No real evidence from most wars that religion is the cause.*

➤ *Religion is certainly involved but not the root cause.*

➤ *Religion often used as a way to drum up support.*

- ➤ *War is contrary to most religious teachings.*
- ➤ *Most wars are not supported by the majority of members of either religion involved but rather extremists who say they represent or are part of them.*
- ➤ *If war was the cause, why are religious sites/people not targeted far more?*

Arguments supporting other views:

- ➤ *The crusades more than likely had religion as their cause.*
- ➤ *If religion was not the cause of war, or one of them, then it would not come to the surface as easily as it does during conflict.*
- ➤ *People do not want to say it is religion because war is often contrary to religious teachings so they cover this cause with other things – but religion as the true cause is soon at the forefront.*
- ➤ *Religions have always disagreed with each other, so it would not be surprising for it to be a cause; it is also something that has divided people at the best of times.*
- ➤ *Some religious teachings encourage war/conflict in order to defend the religion, or the poor or weak – Islam and Sikhism, for example.*

Hints and tips

You need to make sure you give arguments to agree **and** to disagree with the statement – if you give only one point of view, then you cannot get above half marks.

Your answer must be full of religious content – this is a statement about religious beliefs and teachings.

The top level requires good development of the arguments you present. This means giving the argument and explaining clearly why it supports/contradicts the statement using detailed examples. This level is looking for a lot of development.

Try to get into the habit of offering three for and three against arguments in all your AO2 answers. Explain and provide examples for each, and include teachings if possible – this will help push your response to a higher level.

Question 2

Student A

Many Christians believe that they will fight in a war if it is in self-defence or in the defence of others as a last resort if all other avenues have been examined. The whole aim of the war for these believers is to create peace as an outcome. It might be an action seen as a necessary evil. Appropriate rules of war should be followed.

Muslims also have the idea of Jihad – if they are attacked they will defend themselves and others if they are defenceless. It again should be a last resort and peace should be the ultimate aim. If the aggressor at any time wants to talk peace then Muslims have a duty to stop fighting and negotiate that peace. Muslims must fight the war under Just War rules.

🄴 **Both points refer to war being a last resort and acceptable in self-defence and to fight injustice, but also that there are rules to be followed for that war to be clearly just or acceptable. 4 marks**

Question 2
Student B

Some Roman Catholic Christians are pacifists and so won't fight in a war. They believe that Jesus taught a message of love – 'Blessed are the peacemakers' – you can't get much more against war than that!

Some members of the Church of England believe the same principle.

(e) The first point does just enough to get 2 marks and the quotation is very useful here. The second point, although correct, is simply a stated fact rather than a 'simple' explanation. It would not gain any marks as just to say they believe the same thing (even if that is correct) is not worthy of credit.   **2 marks**

Mark scheme

2   Total of 4 marks.

For the first belief given:
- a **simple** explanation of a relevant and accurate point   **(1 mark)**
- a **detailed** explanation of a relevant and accurate point   **(2 marks)**

For the second similar belief given:
- a **simple** explanation of a relevant and accurate point   **(1 mark)**
- a **detailed** explanation of a relevant and accurate point   **(2 marks)**

Answers might include:

General responses – *killing is wrong; all religions teach peace; war is a last resort and must result in a peace being established; Pacifism is a specific belief against war in all circumstances; most religions are prepared to fight although there are rules to follow; reference to a Just War and Holy War may be made.*

Christianity – *Christian teachings focus on peace; Jesus' teaching renounces violence; Christians are told to love their enemies; war only breeds more war; early Christians were pacifists and many are still pacifists today; some Christians accept the need for war in certain circumstances.*

Islam – *Islam means peace, and war should only happen after all peaceful methods have been tried; Muslims have a duty to fight to defend their faith and Allah and to support the weak and oppressed; lesser jihad can be seen as a Holy War so is acceptable.*

Hints and tips

For your second point in your answer, never just state that 'they believe the same', because even if it is true, marks will not be awarded. You must write both parts of your answer fully.

Question 3
Student A

Christians who follow the teachings of Jesus will never use violence in protests. Violence only breeds violence and real peace can only be achieved through dialogue. Hence protests such as demonstrations and marches would be used. Jesus says 'blessed are the peacemakers', and his whole teaching is about love and peace so a good example would be the methods used by Martin Luther King to show what can be achieved if non-violence is adhered to.

Islam encourages peace, but Muslims are taught to do whatever it takes to fight injustice and defend Islam. In the world today, many see Islam and Muslims as under attack and therefore violence has often been turned to, even to the extent of using what others see as terrorism. Shi'a Muslims in particular might use the ideas of Tawalla and Tabarra as reasons to use violence.

ℯ **An excellent answer. Both points have been clearly developed.   4 marks**

Question 3
Student B

Christianity teaches a message of non-violence and many Christians are non-violent pacifists meaning they won't use violence ever.

Muslims will turn to violence if they believe their religion is under attack or to defend injustice. Protests are common, though often turn violent as we see in the media.

ℯ **The first point is a little repetitive, rather than being a developed explanation. The second point, although a valid response, moves away from religious beliefs, and again there is no real development.   2 marks**

Mark scheme

3   Total of 4 marks.

For the first belief given:
   ▷ a **simple** explanation of a relevant and accurate point   (1 mark)
   ▷ a **detailed** explanation of a relevant and accurate point   (2 marks)

For the second contrasting belief given:
   ▷ a **simple** explanation of a relevant and accurate point   (1 mark)
   ▷ a **detailed** explanation of a relevant and accurate point   (2 marks)

Answers might include:

Christianity *– teachings focus on peace and non-violence; Jesus' teachings and actions renounce violence 'those who live by the sword die by the sword'; many Christians have protested using non-violent means, e.g. Martin Luther King. Teachings suggest the love of each other but if non-violent protest is ignored then violence may have to be resorted to. Christians have a duty to protest both individually as a community to issues of unfair treatment, inequality, unjust laws etc.*

Islam – *Islam means peace, but violence can be used in self-defence; there is the duty to protest against injustices and oppression of the weak to restore peace and justice. Many protests do become violent , although this is more about the social climate than following religious beliefs.*

Hints and tips

Check that you are developing your points, rather than repeating the same point in a different way. Examiners will only credit the point made once.

Theme E: Religion, crime and punishment

Question 1

Student A

(a) D: an aim of punishment used to put criminals off crime

(e) **Correct. Deterrence is an aim of punishment whereas the others are definitions of morality, repentance and conscience.   1 mark**

(b) an emotion, like revenge; poverty

(e) **Two clear answers.   2 marks**

(c) Some Christians believe the death penalty for murder is acceptable because in the Old Testament it says 'an eye for an eye' so because a murderer has taken a life then a just punishment is for them to lose their life too. If they are put in prison they often get released and this is not justice because their victim did not get a second chance. The death penalty is like for like.

Other Christians, however, are against the death penalty as they use the teaching of 'Do not kill' from the Commandments. We do not have the right to take away life no matter what a person has done. God gives life and takes it away and there should always be a chance of reform. Also not all murders are the same and should not be judged as the same.

(e) **This is an excellent answer and the use of teachings in each paragraph adds to its quality. One point to be made though is that it is always better to name the specific Christian religions.   4 marks**

(d) Muslims believe that evil comes from a weak human giving in to the temptations of a powerful evil being. The evil being is Iblis, an angel who disobeyed Allah by not bowing to Adam. He was expelled but was able to tempt Adam and Eve to eat the forbidden fruit before they were sent from Eden too. Iblis now carries on tempting humans and we are too weak not to give in so that evil acts in the world.

Christians believe that evil is the abuse of free will that God gave humans and so we have choices in everything to do right or wrong. Also that a devil or Satan figure tries to tempt people constantly to do wrong as he did with Adam and Eve in the Garden of Eden. Evil then is a mix of an external force and an internal failure to do what is right.

(e) Two well written paragraphs. The student clearly understands the origins of evil in both the chosen religions. Although no specific quotes are used both these refer to stories in the holy books.   **5 marks**

(e) Punishment has always been a big dilemma within society in terms of how to punish people, what purpose it serves and how effective it is. If we look at the reoffending rates in the UK, punishment, whatever way it is being carried out, does not seem to be working. Many people are not reformed and neither do they accept the responsibility for what they have done. It could well be argued that the actual punishment has made them worse and bred more hatred and worse people. However, for society to work others would say that there has to be justice and this comes through punishment. It might not stop reoffending but if punishment was not there, then many more would be tempted into crime because they know there is no sanction.

Those who support the statement would also say that in religion there is a great emphasis on forgiveness. Jesus talked about forgiving people not 7 times but 70 x 7 so as many times as necessary – in the same way for the great number of times we ask God to forgive us, we should forgive others. Conversely, others might say that forgiveness has to be earned and that through the punishment process, during the time served, a criminal can show repentance which then allows the victim to show forgiveness, which then allows the victim to see justice has been done, the person has seen the error of what they did and through forgiveness both can move on.

Most people who commit crimes do so for many reasons, which shows that they are victims themselves in some ways, maybe their upbringing, social situation, poverty and while not excuses they are reasons. So we would be far better forgiving and helping them than punishing them. To disagree, people might say that there is always an alternative to crime, they decided to inflict harm on others or their possessions so they have to take the consequences… that is how we learn right from wrong.

In a moral sense it is very easy to have people punished but it is far more difficult to forgive. However the hard way is quite often the right way and also if we forgive, many religions believe we will be rewarded for our actions.

To conclude I feel we need to consider the crime to decide whether forgiveness instead of punishment would be the right way forward. To a mass murderer who has no moral values or respect for life, forgiveness would mean nothing we have to lock them up or else society would not feel protected. At the same time though other criminals could be forgiven and this would be far more beneficial to the criminal and society as a whole. We need to remember that even when we punish, we can forgive, so the two need to go hand in hand. There is some truth in the statement for some crimes, but for others the crime is so terrible, punishment has to be given.

(e) **This student's answer is a good example of what an evaluation answer should look like. It makes clear arguments and each is evaluated. The response concludes with a logical, thoughtful summing up of all the arguments.   L4: 12 marks**

Question 1
Student B

(a) C: a voice inside a person's head putting them off doing bad things

(e) **Incorrect. The correct answer is D: an aim of punishment used to put criminals off crime. Make sure you learn key words and terms.   0 marks**

(b) need money to feed family; debt

(e) **Both these answers are fine – the latter is not in the mark scheme but it is a possible reason for crime.   2 marks**

(c) Islam accepts the death penalty because the Qur'an allows it. A Muslim is not allowed to take life except for justice and where serious laws are broken justice must be done. You can be put to death for things like adultery and blasphemy. It does seem harsh but everyone knows what the law is so they shouldn't break it.

Christians have different beliefs about capital punishment as they use different teachings to support each side – a life for a life and do not kill.

(e) **The student's first paragraph is definitely a developed explanation but the second is not. There is no explanation of the effect of the Christian beliefs, to show full understanding. Although the second paragraph needs more development, the inclusion of the two teachings would gain 1 mark.   3 marks**

(d) Christians can choose to do right and wrong because God gave us free will. Humans often choose the wrong thing because they are tempted by the devil.

Muslims have Iblis who tempts people and humans don't have enough self-discipline to resist him as they are too weak because often to do the right thing is hard.

(e) **Both these are just sufficient as very simple explanations – but there is far more that the student could say to show the examiner greater understanding. There is little reference to teachings – though free will and reference to Iblis may be seen as teachings by examiners. The examiner could see how the answer might have been developed but can only award marks for what has actually been written.   2/3 marks**

(e) A criminal is a person who has broken the law and so the law needs to punish them so that people respect it. Also without that punishment people would never learn the difference between right and wrong and society would be chaos. Punishment shows that justice has been done and the victim can find closure and move on with their lives. When people are punished many do see what they did wrong and how they hurt their victims and so want to say sorry. When they get to this point, victims can often forgive whereas if the criminal is not punished they will simply keep offending and hurting other people. Also if someone is dangerous we have to punish otherwise they would probably kill again. It does not make sense to not punish.

However others might say that for every one person that punishment works for and so they never do it again, there are too many for whom it makes them worse. Prison is like a school for criminals and they learn how to do worse things. Putting all those bad people in one place, how can we expect them to turn their lives around? Also all religions say we should forgive as God forgives us when we ask. Also I think he forgives us even when we don't.

Overall I believe that we need both in place. Some criminals and the reasons for their crimes are more understandable and so we can see that punishment might not work for them, but for others forgiveness might not be easy.

(e) **This student's first paragraph contains many reasons for forgiveness of wrongdoing and it would be good to have seen some of these developed a little more. The response reads a little too much like AO1 not AO2. The ideas are valid and many of them are the same as those in Student A's response, but the writing lacks the development and evaluation which shows real understanding. Some explanation of what religious teachings say would have been better too. The conclusion is sensible, but again could have been explained further.   L3: 8 marks**

Mark scheme

1   **(a)** 1 mark for the correct answer.

The correct answer is D: an aim of punishment used to put criminals off crime

Hints and tips

These questions usually rely entirely on knowledge of key words and terms – you need to learn them.

Be careful to read the question carefully as it could ask you what something IS or what it IS NOT.

(b) 1 mark per correct answer, up to 2 marks maximum.

Answers might include:

Umbrella terms such as: upbringing, mental illness, poverty, addiction, greed, hate, opposition to existing laws.

Specific answers such as: the need for money, peer pressure, feed a habit, anger, revenge etc.

Hints and tips

Do not explain anything unless instructed to – just give two words or phrases to answer this question. That frees up your time to answer later questions.

The language of questions is really important. For this topic, 'types', 'causes', 'reasons', 'effects' and 'consequences' are all words that could be used by the examiner. Make sure you understand what each term is asking for, as if you mix them up you are throwing easy marks away.

(c) Total of 4 marks.

For the first belief given:
 – a **simple** explanation of a relevant and accurate point   **(1 mark)**
 – a **detailed** explanation of a relevant and accurate point   **(2 marks)**

For the second contrasting belief given:
 – a **simple** explanation of a relevant and accurate point   **(1 mark)**
 – a **detailed** explanation of a relevant and accurate point   **(2 marks)**

Answers might include:

Christianity – *generally does not support the death penalty. The Church of England was at the forefront of the move to end its use in the UK. It is seen as a breach of the commandment 'Do not kill',* *because a life is being deliberately ended. It also denies the sanctity of life as the life of the criminal can be taken, and is against their human dignity. There is no chance of reform of this person as death is final.*

Some Christians believe it is right to use the death penalty for those criminals who have committed the worst crimes, such as murder. Since they have taken life, they forfeit their own – 'An eye for an eye' (Exodus 21:24).

***Islamic (Shariah) Law** – includes the use of capital punishment. The Qur'an states the crimes which are punishable by death (5:32). The Qur'an insists 'Take not life except by way of justice and law', so the crime must be sufficient. Also there is the 'Law of Compensation' that can be applied – to show mercy is greatly valued and rewarded in Islam so the victims can be offered the chance of no death penalty if compensation is paid. A lesser punishment would still have to be served.*

Hints and tips

You have to give two **different** beliefs in the answer to this question – writing about one can only get you 2 out of 4 marks.

Always read the whole question including the instructions as this could be vital to prevent a wasted answer.

(d) Total of 4 marks + 1 mark

Look for explanation of two different teachings in the answer.

For the first teaching given:
- a **simple** explanation of a teaching which is both clearly relevant to the question and accurate **(1 mark)**
- a **detailed** explanation of a teaching which is both clearly relevant to the question and accurate **(2 marks)**

For the second teaching given:
- a **simple** explanation of a teaching which is both clearly relevant to the question and accurate **(1 mark)**
- a **detailed** explanation of a teaching which is both clearly relevant to the question and accurate **(2 marks)**

Relevant and accurate reference to scripture and/or sacred writing as required. **(1 mark)**

Answers might include:

***Christianity** – believes in a figure called the devil or Satan, who is an evil power, though ultimately less powerful than God. The devil continually tries to tempt people and encourage them to behave badly. So, evil is a combination of internal and external factors.*

***Islam** – the Qur'an says that there is a devil who was an angel. Allah had ordered the angels to bow to Adam, but Iblis refused. Iblis was expelled from paradise, but was able to cause Adam and Eve's expulsion from Eden. Iblis continually tempts and pushes humans to be wicked. Humans fail to show self-discipline, and give in to Iblis' temptations. Evil, therefore, is a mix of a powerful evil being and the weakness of humans.*

Hints and tips

You have to explain two **different** teachings in the answer to this question.

The mark scheme tells you that the points have to be 'clearly relevant' – if you write something that does not make sense, or that you have to think about to make it relevant, then it is not a good answer.

A good way to answer is to give a teaching, and then explain how it is important.

You do not have to give exact quotations – it is fine to paraphrase. What you have to do is make it obvious that you are referring to something a person definitely said, and that what you say they said is approximately right. This is especially true when you are referring to a long teaching.

Try and learn specific teachings as they serve your argument much better and show greater knowledge than using generic ones everywhere.

(e) These questions are marked according to levels of response – this means your answer is judged for its quality overall, not for how many different arguments you present.

Answers might include:

Arguments in support of the view:

➤ *Punishment does not work whether it is a positive or negative one – reoffending figures clearly show this.*

➤ *Punishment breads hatred and negative emotions.*

➤ *Jesus says forgive not 7 times but 70 x 7, the Qur'an says whoever forgives and makes up with another will be rewarded by Allah, Judaism forbids people to take revenge, Buddhism sees forgiveness as showing two virtues – compassion and understanding, Sikhism believes forgiveness is as essential to life as food, Hinduism sees forgiveness as one of the cardinal virtues.*

➤ *Forgiveness is the far greater moral response than the revenge idea of punishment.*

➤ *Victims feel better and able to move on if they can forgive whereas seeing the criminal punished does not always have the same effect.*

➤ *Humans expect God to forgive them so they should be able to forgive others.*

➤ *Forgiveness is compassionate whereas punishment is vengeful.*

➤ *Forgiveness does not mean the crime is forgotten.*

Arguments supporting other views:

➤ *Although forgiveness is important, justice when the law is broken is also important.*

➤ *Punishment is necessary for any system to work.*

➤ *Punishment is a process which allows repentance and therefore others are able to forgive.*

➤ *If punishments did not exist society would be chaos.*

➤ *Rather than applying to everyone, punishment could be dependent upon the crime attitude of the criminal and reasons for the crime.*

Hints and tips

You need to make sure you give arguments to agree **and** to disagree with the statement – if you give only one point of view, then you cannot get above half marks.

Your answer must be full of religious content – this is a statement about religious beliefs and teachings.

The top level requires good development of the arguments you present. This means giving the argument and explaining clearly why it supports/contradicts the statement using detailed examples. This level is looking for a lot of development.

Try to get into the habit of offering three for and three against arguments in all your AO2 answers. Explain and provide examples for each, and include teachings if possible – this will help push your response to a higher level.

Question 2
Student A

Christians would say that reformation is the key to helping criminals. The majority will return to society at some point so if they see the error of their ways and reform then this is the best outcome for society. Christians believe that many can be reformed through education, counselling and go on to not offend again. Quakers would say there is a part of God in everyone so everyone is redeemable.

Muslims also believe in reformation but through a different route. They give out harsh punishments like lashings and removal of limbs and as a result criminals reform because they have learned that their behaviour is not tolerated.

ⓔ **A good answer. Both points are clearly stated and have a developed explanation. The similarity here is in the belief, even though the way of reformation is different.   4 marks**

Question 2
Student B

Buddhism believes that everyone has Buddha nature so everyone can be reformed if we help them to know the real consequences of their behaviour.

The Church of England believes that reformation is important because it lead the campaign for prison reform in Britain which includes programmes to make prisoners better people.

ⓔ **Two simple explanations are given here. Both are a little weak but are valid responses, and are more than simply stating a point.   2 marks**

Mark scheme

2   Total of 4 marks.

For the first belief given:
> a **simple** explanation of a relevant and accurate point   (1 mark)
> a **detailed** explanation of a relevant and accurate point   (2 marks)

For the second similar belief given:
> a **simple** explanation of a relevant and accurate point   (1 mark)
> a **detailed** explanation of a relevant and accurate point   (2 marks)

Answers might include:
All religions agree with reformation but in different ways.

Harsh punishments as well as good treatment lead to reform. Christians and Buddhists believe reformation can come from positive help programmes, whereas in Islam, Shari'ah law suggests that people can learn their lesson through the punishment given.

Hindus believe in reformation as it will help them on their path to enlightenment.

Judaism says love your neighbour in Leviticus, so to apply a reform programme would be seeing this in action.

Sikhism says reformation is when light is brought to the darkness.

Hints and tips

Remember, similarities in belief might well prove different in practice but they are still an acceptable answer.

Question 3
Student A

In Christianity many believe that 'evil' has to exist because 'good' exists and one cannot be understood without the other. It is a just part of nature, just what happens, and see things as one or the other. Its existence makes us appreciate what is good.

Other Christians would say that God gave humans free will so that humanity is not like His puppets. We have choices in everything we do – God knows the choices we make and are going to make before we do them, but He allows us to make those choices. Humans have a lack of self-discipline to do what is good so evil is not connected with God but is a fact of human existence and choice.

e **The two points have a developed explanation for 2 marks each. The last sentence needs to be further explained to make total sense but enough has been written up to that point to gain the marks.   4 marks**

Question 3
Student B

Islam says that a devil was an evil angel. He was called Iblis and tempts and pushes humans to be wicked. Humans give into Iblis too easily and so there is a lot of evil.

Some Christians believe you have to have evil if you have good, so both exist.

e **The first point is a simple and correct explanation, but the second point does not quite have enough detail.   2 marks**

Mark scheme

3   Total of 4 marks.

For the first belief given:
▷ a **simple** explanation of a relevant and accurate point   (1 mark)
▷ a **detailed** explanation of a relevant and accurate point   (2 marks)

For the second contrasting belief given:
▷ a **simple** explanation of a relevant and accurate point   (1 mark)
▷ a **detailed** explanation of a relevant and accurate point   (2 marks)

Answers might include:

Christianity – *evil is an abuse of free will which is given by God; in order to see good, evil has to exist; the Devil tries to tempt people to behave badly as he did with Adam and Eve in the Garden of Eden through the serpent tempting them to eat from the prohibited tree of knowledge.*

Islam – *the devil was an evil angel called Iblis who refused to bow to Adam and so was expelled from Eden – he tempts and pushes humans to be wicked; humans give into Iblis too easily and so there is a lot of evil; evil is a mix of powerful evil and the weakness of humans.*

Hints and tips

On some topics it is easy to write too much, so be careful in how much you write to avoid wasting time that you do not have.

Theme F: Religion, human rights and social justice

Question 1
Student A

(a) C: people traffickers

ⓔ **Correct.   1 mark**

(b) Free speech and an education.

ⓔ **Two rights clearly identified.   2 marks**

(c) Although Christian churches differ in their interpretation of the status of women in the different churches, the Bible is quite definite. Paul taught 'there is neither Jew nor Greek, male or female… for you are all one in Jesus Christ'. This seems to suggest the idea of equality as do the facts that it was women that Jesus appeared to after his resurrection, the first people to be baptised as Christians were women, and the leaders of some of the early Christian communities were women. Therefore some Christian groups allow women to become vicars because they are equally capable.

The Roman Catholic Church, though, takes the words of Timothy which suggest that women 'could not teach or have authority over a man' so while they could pray publicly they were not allowed to lead. The Catholics therefore do not allow women to be priests in the churches. They respect women but the priesthood is male only.

ⓔ **This is a good answer – the student explains two contrasting views within the Christian religion and uses teachings to support these views.   4 marks**

(d) In Islam Muslims are taught 'he who eats and drinks whilst his brother goes hungry is not one of us' meaning that you cannot call yourself a Muslim if you have plenty and see others go hungry. This along with the practice of Sadaqah teaches Muslims that they should tackle poverty and it is what Allah would want them to do as a community both in the UK and abroad.

Christians are told the story of the rich man and Lazarus the beggar. He sat at the rich man's gate and was ignored each day and when they both died the rich man found himself in Hell and saw Lazarus in Heaven. This indicates that Christians should tackle poverty literally at their own front door and that they will be rewarded for that help. For those who don't there will be punishment. Poverty in the UK is an issue which Christians should respond to.

ⓔ Both teachings are excellently explained and applied to the question.   5 marks

(e) Some people might begin this by asking 'what exactly do we mean by wealthy?' Also where do we cross the line for wealth to be unacceptable? These ideas are key to this question because it is quite often the case that others might see someone as wealthy whereas they themselves might not. Some would say that it is not wrong to be wealthy if the wealth has been earned honestly and through hard work because then the wealth is deserved, yet others might say well there are many people who work equally as hard yet don't have that wealth. There is such a vast gulf between the rich and poor that it is feels immoral that such wealth exists yet others don't even have clean water. However, the rich might well donate millions to help yet the problem still exists, as money cannot control the weather or disease or wars.

Many religions would disagree with the statement because generally the belief is that is it fine to be wealthy to the extent that some even see it as a blessing from God. 'Humans are caretakers of Allah's wealth' and Christians believe wealth is a gift from God. What is wrong is when there becomes a love of this money and a desire for more, beyond the far more important things in life like family, God and worship. It is the greedy that are condemned not the riches themselves. Christians believe the 'love of money is the root of all evil' and Christians should 'be on guard against all kinds of greed, a man's life does not consist in the abundance of his possessions…'. Islam says that people who seek money out of greed are like people who eat but are never full and also in the Hadith it states that 'it is not poverty that I fear for you but that you may begin to desire the world as others have and it might destroy you as it destroyed them'. This a very strong message for Muslims to receive, that greed is worse than poverty. Others would say the statement is true because with all of these religious views there is the clear warning that too much money does ruin people and we only have to look at many lottery winners where the money has destroyed their lives.

Many would say that with wealth comes responsibility and if we see rich people using their money in a way which we see as good for others then we tend not to have an issue with the fact they are rich. Most religions add this proviso onto the idea that it is not wrong to be rich as long as the money is used in the right way – so not greedy, not excessive buying of material goods, not spending for spending sake but using it to benefit others. Conversely though, if people work hard why should they spend it on others? We need to see here that there are double standards and judgements being made all the time on this issue. Just because Bill Gates gives £1 billion to Africa every year – does that make it okay for him to be so wealthy? For many it does but in reality he is so wealthy that giving billions has little impact on him. It would take a vast redistribution of the wealth and resources of the whole world's issues to even out the world's wealth which may not even be possible.

The crux of this question for me is not whether wealth is wrong but more about how it is earned and how it is used. There will always be wealthy and poorer people, unselfish and selfish – this is a fact of human life and some wealth we object to and others we don't. Wealth itself is not wrong but more the thoughts and desires that go with it.

ⓔ This is a superb answer which threads evaluation all the way through it. It even widens the question too with its examples and religious teachings. A very thorough, logical and reasoned piece of writing.   L4: 12 marks

Question 1
Student B

(a) government, charities, religious groups

(e) **Incorrect. The correct answer is C: people traffickers. Be careful to read the question carefully as it could ask you what something IS or what it IS NOT.   0 marks**

(b) People have rights under the UN Declaration such as free speech which means that people can say what they want and they have rights to food, water, shelter and healthcare because we all need these to survive.

(e) **Two rights are correctly identified but time is wasted explaining what they are. The first explanation is in fact incorrect but the identified 'right' of free speech is correct and no explanation is required by the question.   2 marks**

(c) In the Orthodox church women are highly respected as they are given a role by God – to have children and be a mother. If they were priests then the interpretation is that they couldn't be good mothers as well as it would distract them from this so the leaders are all male.

In Islam all the Pillars and obligations apply to women but they cannot lead prayers in the mosque unless it is in the women's section only, as then the prayers for men and boys would be invalid.

(e) **Both these ideas need a little more explanation through the use of more detail or even an example. Without this detail they remain at the 'simple' level of development.   2 marks**

(d) Christians believe if you help others it is like helping Jesus so they should tackle poverty and Muslims are taught that they are not really Muslims if they don't help people so they should tackle poverty.

(e) **This student identifies two correct teachings but fails to explain them. The explanation in this case just repeats the question ('so they should tackle poverty') and does not show any understanding of the teaching.   2 marks**

(e) Many people would agree that it is wrong to be wealthy in the modern world because there are so many people who are poor. Many have more wealth than they can ever use while others are starving. Many would say that the rich are greedy, for example the lottery winner who won the jackpot and then bought another ticket for the week after… and won again! They spend their wealth only on themselves like ten sports cars or a massive house that they don't need. Even if they have worked hard I think this is wrong. Christians say that God expects them to use the luxury of their wealth to help others.

Others might say that wealth is a blessing from God and that is it not wrong especially if they have worked for it. God wants to see what we do with it and if good is done with it like giving to charity then this is more acceptable. And also no one is really wealthy because it all belongs to God anyway – we just look after it when we are here – a kind of test to see how we manage it from God.

I do and don't agree with the statement really. I don't agree because being wealthy depends on so many different things and it's not a simple issue, but I do agree because some wealth is massively excessive and just handed down and they have so much they don't know what to do with it when other people are dying in poverty.

ⓔ The question raises an emotive issue – as questions of money always do – and this student obviously has strong feelings. However, the level of answer he/she gives is quite simple in terms of arguments and religious teachings. There is a range of points but because they are simply made the answer stays below L3. Note that the conclusion is weak – the student does not sum up the arguments beyond restating the fact that there are two sides to the argument. This is not a good structure to use in this context.   **L2: 6 marks**

Mark scheme

1   **(a)** 1 mark for the correct answer.

The correct answer is C: people traffickers

Hints and tips

These questions usually rely entirely on knowledge of key words and terms – you need to learn them.

Be careful to read the question carefully as it could ask you what something IS or what it IS NOT.

(b) 1 mark per correct answer, up to 2 marks maximum.

Answers might include:

Everyone is equal, born free, should be treated in the same way and is innocent until proven guilty.

Everyone should respect everyone else.

Everyone has the right to: legal protection, a public trial, asylum, belong to a country, marry, own things and keep them, free speech, meet peacefully with others, vote, work, rest, an education, basic rights – water, food, shelter, healthcare, artistic freedom and enjoy the arts.

No one should be: tortured, unfairly imprisoned.

No one may destroy the rights of other.

There must be laws to protect these rights.

Hints and tips

Do not explain anything unless instructed to – just give two words or phrases to answer this question. That frees up your time to answer later questions.

(c) Total of 4 marks.

For the first belief given:
- a **simple** explanation of a relevant and accurate point   (1 mark)
- a **detailed** explanation of a relevant and accurate point   (2 marks)

For the second contrasting belief given:
- a **simple** explanation of a relevant and accurate point   (1 mark)
- a **detailed** explanation of a relevant and accurate point   (2 marks)

Answers might include:

*Women have status in **Christianity**. Christians believe that God made people free and equal – in the image of God (Genesis 1:27). St Paul said: 'There is neither Jew nor Greek, male nor* *female, for you are all one in Christ Jesus' (Galatians 3:28) – demonstrating equality. The first people to see Jesus after his resurrection were female, and early church leaders included women.*

*In the **Roman Catholic Church**, women may not hold positions of authority. While women could publicly pray and prophesy in church, they could not teach or have authority over a man (1 Tim. 2:11–14). These are two essential functions of the clergy, so women are scripturally excluded from these roles.*

*In **Islam**, whilst a woman may study the Qur'an and Islamic jurisprudence, they may not lead the mosque, as prayers for men and boys would not be valid. Hadith states 'a nation that appoints a woman as its ruler shall never prosper' (Bukhari). The Qur'an states that women have rights, but men have the final word and so greater status (Qur'an 2:229).*

*In the **Orthodox Church**, women may not have leadership roles. Women have a God-given role and task as a mother, and nothing is more important than this role. Nothing must be allowed to detract from it either, even priesthood.*

Hints and tips

You have to give two **different** beliefs in the answer to this question – writing about one can only get you 2 out of 4 marks. Always read the whole question including the instructions as this could be vital to prevent a wasted answer.

(d) Total of 4 marks + 1 mark

Look for explanation of two different teachings in the answer.

For the first teaching given:

– a **simple** explanation of a teaching which is both clearly relevant to the question and accurate   **(1 mark)**

– a **detailed** explanation of a teaching which is both clearly relevant to the question and accurate   **(2 marks)**

For the second teaching given:

– a **simple** explanation of a teaching which is both clearly relevant to the question and accurate   **(1 mark)**

– a **detailed** explanation of a teaching which is both clearly relevant to the question and accurate   **(2 marks)**

Relevant and accurate reference to scripture and/or sacred writing as required.   **(1 mark)**

Answers might include:

Christianity *– 'if anyone has material possessions and sees his brother in need how can the love of God be in him?' (1 John 3:17). 'If a brother has no clothes or food what good is it to wish him well without caring for his physical needs?' (James 2:15) 'You shall not burden your heart or shut your hand against your poor brother' (Old Testament). Jesus spent most of his time ministering to people who today would be considered to be the poor and many of his parables are about how his listeners should respond to those around them that society has set aside.*

Islam *– 'He who eats and drinks whilst his brother goes hungry is not one of us' (Hadith). 'For a debtor, give him time to pay – but if you let it go out of charity this is the best thing to do' (Qur'an).*

Hints and tips

You have to explain two **different** teachings in the answer to this question.

The mark scheme tells you that the points have to be 'clearly relevant' – if you write something that does not make sense, or that you have to think about to make it relevant, then it is not a good answer.

A good way to answer is to give a teaching, and then explain how it is important.

You do not have to give exact quotations – it is fine to paraphrase. What you have to do is make it obvious that you are referring to something a person definitely said, and that what you say they said is approximately right. This is especially true when you are referring to a long teaching.

Try and learn specific teachings as they serve your argument much better and show greater knowledge than using generic ones everywhere.

(e) These questions are marked according to levels of response – this means your answer is judged for its quality overall, not for how many different arguments you present.

Answers might include:

Arguments in support of view:

➤ *It is wrong if wealth has become a desire and more important than other things.*
➤ *It is wrong as it leads to temptations and ruin as people strive for it.*
➤ *It is wrong because it can make people selfish.*
➤ *Focus on wealth means less focus on God/worship.*
➤ *The love of money is the root of all evil.*
➤ *Material possessions mean nothing – happiness is far more important.*
➤ *It is wrong when half the world's people have nothing.*
➤ *Leads to needless and worthless spending.*

Arguments supporting other views:

➤ *It depends on what wealthy means.*
➤ *If it is earned legally and through hard work why not be wealthy?*
➤ *If a person is wealthy they can do much to help others.*
➤ *Wealth is seen by many religions as a blessing from God.*
➤ *To be wealthy is not wrong – but it is a test.*
➤ *No one is wealthy because everything belongs to God – it is just on loan to us.*
➤ *Nothing is wrong essentially with wealth, it is what we do with it.*

Hints and tips

You need to make sure you give arguments to agree **and** to disagree with the statement – if you give only one point of view, then you cannot get above half marks.

Your answer must be full of religious content – this is a statement about religious beliefs and teachings.

The top level requires good development of the arguments you present. This means giving the argument and explaining clearly why it supports/contradicts the statement using detailed examples. This level is looking for a lot of development.

Try to get into the habit of offering three for and three against arguments in all your AO2 answers. Explain and provide examples for each, and include teachings if possible – this will help push your response to a higher level.

Question 2

Student A

The Church of England supports Christian Aid because they help some of the poorest people in the world. They do this to follow the example of Jesus who spent most of his ministry on Earth helping the poor and outcasts of society.

Muslims will give to charity through Sadaqah and when disasters occur Muslim charities are then able to help the people facing such disasters like flooding or earthquakes. They do this because their teachings say 'cure poverty with charity and give generously'.

ⓔ **The first developed point looks at giving in a specific way, i.e. to a specific charity, while the second discusses giving in general and the principles behind it.   4 marks**

Question 2

Student B

Christians believe in love your neighbour so they give to different charities, for example after a disaster or they give a donation monthly to a chosen charity. All this shows a love for others in different places in the world, Christian or not.

ⓔ **This answer only explains one point so it can only achieve a maximum of 2 marks.   2 marks**

Mark scheme

2   Total of 4 marks.

For the first belief given:
> a **simple** explanation of a relevant and accurate point   (1 mark)
> a **detailed** explanation of a relevant and accurate point   (2 marks)

For the second similar belief given:
> a **simple** explanation of a relevant and accurate point   (1 mark)
> a **detailed** explanation of a relevant and accurate point   (2 marks)

Answers might include:

All religions believe in helping those less fortunate out of compassion, or following religious teachings, or following the example of religious leaders.
Giving to charity earns rewards, either towards good karma or for a place in heaven.
Charities also fight injustices and all religions promote this.
Helping the poor is a specific part of religious belief and being a member of that religion.

Hints and tips

Always think of charity in the widest sense – so it can involve giving to an organisation, giving as an individual or religious group, or it could also involve doing a job, giving time and expertise and not just money.

Question 3
Student A

In Islam, Sunni Muslims give 2.5% of their wealth in zakah each year. This is a welfare contribution, but it is compulsory. It goes to the poor and needy. It is a duty – they MUST pay it.

Shi'a Muslims pay zakah, but they also pay khums, which is 20% of their profit each year, a big part of which goes to the poor and needy. They give more. It is one of the Ten Obligations of Shi'a Islam, so they MUST also do both.

(e) **This is a good answer as it is not easy to find differences on this topic. Both differences are clearly stated and have a developed explanation. 4 marks**

Question 3
Student B

Some Christians tithe for charity. They give 10% of their earnings.

Most Christians give to charity when they see something that makes them feel they should help, because they follow the teaching of 'Love your neighbour'.

(e) **Both the points given are valid, but the explanation is limited for each, so marks are only awarded for a 'simple' explanation. 2 marks**

Mark scheme

3   Total of 4 marks.

For the first belief given:
> a **simple** explanation of a relevant and accurate point   (1 mark)
> a **detailed** explanation of a relevant and accurate point   (2 marks)

For the second contrasting belief given:
> a **simple** explanation of a relevant and accurate point   (1 mark)
> a **detailed** explanation of a relevant and accurate point   (2 marks)

Answers might include:

General responses *– all religions encourage the giving of money, gifts, time etc. to charity; where there are differences it may be in the nature of the charity supported (for example, not supporting a charity which is at odds with their moral code), or in how much to support it (for example, whether by a fixed amount linked to duty, or freely).*

Christianity *– Love your neighbour; the Parable of the Rich Man and Lazarus; Jesus' example of helping those in need; the idea of giving what you have extra to those in need – following Jesus; there are many Christian charities; tithing is a norm in some Christian traditions as is giving a fixed amount to charity in others.*

Islam *– zakah; khums; sadaqah; anyone who sees his brother in need and does not help is not a Muslim – Muhammad; the existence of many Muslim charities for the poor, and that a number of Muslim countries are less economically developed suggests support for giving to the poor.*

Paper 2A Thematic Studies
Sample set 2

Theme A: Relationships and families

Question 1
Student A

(a) B: a relationship between two men

ⓔ **Correct. They are all types of relationship except the last one which does not exist. Answer C is not allowed by law in the UK but a religion might practise it unofficially. This is a starter question where each answer needs reading carefully as it is easy to make a mistake. This student read it carefully and gave the correct answer.   1 mark**

(b) For love and to have sex in a legal relationship.

ⓔ **Two clear ideas.   2 marks**

(c) One contrasting view about contraception is from the Roman Catholic tradition. They believe that any act of sex should be open to allowing procreation so any form of artificial contraception is unacceptable but natural methods could be used because it still allows natural law to take place. The Pope actually said contraception was 'evil'.

The Anglican Church believes that the act of sex is a good thing in itself because it is an expression of love so the result is not always the key issue. They believe that there could be good reasons for delaying a couple becoming parents and this is sensible. So it is not a sin.

ⓔ **This answer offers two clearly contrasting denominational views, both of which are explained.   4 marks**

(d) In the Bible it says 'there is neither Jew nor Greek, slave or free men, male or female as you are all one in Christ'. This means that to discriminate on the grounds of gender would be going against this teaching. In Christ everyone is equal so this is true for both male and female, so for example if women are treated differently at work by being paid less for the same job as a man then this is against what the Bible teaches.

Also at the start of Christianity when Jesus had gone to heaven and the disciples started to go out and spread the faith, women were converted and preached. Two of the first baptised converts were women and Priscilla was the leader of the church in Ephesus. This shows that if women were leaders then, Churches today who don't allow women to lead could be said to be wrong — they were leaders then, so why not now.

ⓔ **This answer is focused entirely on Christianity, but this is fine as no specific instruction was given in the question. The student gives two clear Bible references, the first a quote and the second a Biblical example. They are both explained and show clear understanding.   5 marks**

(e) On reading this question we need to look at two issues really: first whether only heterosexual couples should have children as opposed to homosexual or single-parent families and second whether the heterosexual couples should have to be married. Most religions do not believe in sex before marriage and as sex is required to have children then this would imply that children should be born within marriage. Religions mainly recognise heterosexual marriage only, so this would agree with the statement. The Bible says that God made man and woman and told them to populate the earth, so this suggests that sex between man and woman is what was designed as being natural. Also as married couples have made a commitment to each other, then marriage is a more stable place to bring up children. Marriage makes children legitimate under the law and traditionally and naturally children are born to a male/female couple. Roman Catholics teaching is against sex before marriage and homosexuality so the only place for children to be born is within marriage, to a heterosexual couple.

In earlier times this statement was undoubtedly true, however in the modern world there are many different types of families and science has made it possible for children to be conceived differently. If God did not support this then would He have allowed scientists the ability to produce such techniques? Just because someone is homosexual does not mean that they want children any less and surely science should be embraced because any child would be very much wanted. In comparison where children are born into marriage they are not always wanted – it might be carelessness – whereas for a homosexual couple or single person conception is a very deliberate act. Also being married does not guarantee they stay together and then the child is caught up in a difficult divorce and just because they are married does not guarantee either that they will make good parents.

I feel that it should not be a matter of the nature of the couple but how much they actually want to be parents, or a parent, that is important. It is obvious that a heterosexual married couple is the natural and traditional way, but as in anything in life, things change and I believe religions should change with them. Buddhism talks about the nature of the relationship being loving as being important, not about the nature or status of the people involved. There can be difficulties in any relationship and marriage may well be the best place for children but in fact any couple can want and love children as can an individual and it is this love that in my opinion is most important.

(e) **A well-argued answer which is clearly focused on the question. Much evaluation is shown through the variety of ideas on either side of the statement. The answer flows from one linked idea to another; it is logical and comes to a reasoned conclusion.   L4: 12 marks**

Question 1
Student B

(a) A: a relationship between a man and a woman

(e) **Incorrect. The correct answer is B: a relationship between two men. Make sure you read the question and the key word carefully.   0 marks**

(b) Because the family expect you to as maybe it is traditional in that culture.

(e) **This student leaves the examiner to make a decision – is this answer two ideas, or is the first idea being explained further? It is easy to see the second part simply as explanation of the first idea rather than a separate idea. Be careful to provide two clear ideas.   1 mark**

(c) Muslims, who are a major group in Great Britain, believe that a couple should practise responsible parenthood. They are allowed to use contraception as long as they agree on this as a couple but their use should not be long term or the contraception permanent. They should be able to care for the children they have.

Jews, who are also a big religion in Great Britain, use contraception for medical or health reasons, e.g. if the mother has a heart condition. Jews talk about the wasting of the seed so the Pill, for example, should not be used because the sperm has no chance of fertilising the egg.

ⓔ This student gives two clear and developed answers but the question says 'refer to the main religious tradition in Great Britain i.e. Christianity or a Christian denomination. Only one of these responses can therefore be marked by the examiner, representing the 'one other' religious tradition asked for in the question. Always read the question carefully.   2 marks

(d) Christians believe in equality that God 'created mankind in his own image' so women and men should be equal. Also Jesus says that 'we are all one in Christ' so if we are all one how can we be separated?

ⓔ This answer has two ideas within it but neither is developed. More explanation is needed to convince the examiner that the student fully understands the point being made and more of a direct connection to the question about 'gender discrimination would have made a much better response. There is a correct reference to a quote so credit is given for this.   3 marks

(e) The Bible says that man and woman (Adam and Eve) should fill the earth so from the very beginning it was about a heterosexual couple having children. This was what God designed and instructed. Most religions do not believe that sex should take place anywhere other than in marriage so with these two ideas the statement in the question appears correct. Also if the couple remarried they must love each other and are more stable than an unmarried couple who could walk away from each other too easily. Also Islam teaches that homosexuality is an offence that a person should be put to death for, so they would also agree with the statement. People are not allowed sex before marriage either which would agree with the statement.

However there are many people who would say that it is not important whether the couple is married or whether they are straight or gay, it is more important that they really want the child. Many gay couples and single parents make superb parents whereas many married male and female couples do a terrible job as parents. Other relationships are now becoming more common and acceptable. We live in a modern world and religion needs to adjust to the changes. Medical science makes it possible for alternative couples to have children and as God gives scientists the talent this must be OK.

ⓔ This student offers a number of interesting ideas, but the response is superficial in that it is more of a list of ideas than an evaluation with arguments for and against the statements. It is marked on the border between L2 and L3.   L2/3: 6/7 marks

Mark scheme

1   (a) 1 mark for the correct answer.

The correct answer is B: a relationship between two men

Hints and tips

These questions usually rely entirely on knowledge of key words and terms – you need to learn them.

Be careful to read the question carefully as it could ask you what something IS or what it IS NOT.

(b) 1 mark per correct answer, up to 2 marks maximum.

Answers might include:

to show love for another person, to make the couple's relationship legitimate, to have children within a legal relationship, religious duty, family expectations, for sex, for financial reasons, for money, for companionship.

Hints and tips

Do not explain anything unless instructed to – just give two words or phrases to answer this question. That frees up your time to answer later questions.

The language of questions is really important. For this topic, 'types', 'causes', 'reasons', 'effects' and 'consequences' are all words that could be used by the examiner. Make sure you understand what each term is asking for, as if you mix them up you are throwing easy marks away.

(c) Total of 4 marks.

For the first belief given:
- for a **simple** explanation of a relevant and accurate point (1 mark)
- for a **detailed** explanation of a relevant and accurate point (2 marks)

For the second contrasting belief given:
- for a **simple** explanation of a relevant and accurate point (1 mark)
- for a **detailed** explanation of a relevant and accurate point (2 marks)

Answers might include:

Catholic Christianity *– all sex open to procreation as this is natural law, Pope declared contraception evil, artificial contraception usage is a deliberate act so sinful, to go against Catholic teaching by choice or circumstance is to disobey Catholic teaching.*

Islam *– Muhammad taught responsible parenthood, by agreement between the couple, non-permanent methods only, should want children when the time is right as children are a purpose of marriage, couple should only have the children they can care for.*

Hints and tips

You have to give two **different** ways in which religious beliefs/teachings influence modern British society in the answer to this question – writing about one way can only get you 2 out of 4 marks.

Always read the whole question including the instructions as this could be vital to prevent a wasted answer.

(d) Total of 4 marks + 1 mark

Look for explanation of two different teachings in the answer.

For the first teaching given:
- a **simple** explanation of a teaching which is both clearly relevant to the question and accurate (1 mark)
- a **detailed** explanation of a teaching which is both clearly relevant to the question and accurate (2 marks)

For the second teaching given:
- a **simple** explanation of a teaching which is both clearly relevant to the question and accurate (1 mark)

– a **detailed** explanation of a teaching which is both clearly relevant to the question and accurate **(2 marks)**

Relevant and accurate reference to scripture and/or sacred writing as required. **1 mark**. Answers might include:

Christianity – *some of the earliest converts, and leaders of Churches were women, for example Priscilla at Ephesus. 'There is neither Jew nor Gentile, neither slave nor free, nor is there male and female, for you are all one in Christ Jesus' (Galatians 3:28). 'So God created mankind in His own image, in the image of God He created them; male and female he created them' (Genesis 1:27).*

Islam – *men and women have the same spiritual nature, according to the Qur'an. Prophet Muhammad said: 'I commend you to be kind to women', 'I shall not lose sight of the labour of any of you who labours in My way, be it man or woman; each of you is equal to the other' (Qur'an 3:195).*

Hints and tips

You have to explain two **different** teachings in the answer to this question.

The mark scheme tells you that the points have to be 'clearly relevant' – if you write something that does not make sense, or that you have to think about to make it relevant, then it is not a good answer.

A good way to answer is to give a teaching, and then explain how it is important.

You do not have to give exact quotations – it is fine to paraphrase. What you have to do is make it obvious that you are referring to something a person definitely said, and that what you say they said is approximately right. This is especially true when you are referring to a long teaching.

Using key technical terms is always very impressive to the examiner. Try to make sure you use them when you can.

(e) These questions are marked according to levels of response – this means your answer is judged for its quality overall, not for how many different arguments you present.

Answers might include:

Arguments in support of the view:

➤ *Sex before marriage is not allowed in many religions so the couple, if having sex to have children, should be married.*

➤ *More stable relationship to bring children into as the couple are committed to each other.*

➤ *God told male and female to reproduce so the couple should be heterosexual.*

➤ *Heterosexual sex is natural.*

Arguments supporting other views:

➤ *It does not matter who is having the child as long as the child is wanted and loved.*

➤ *Being married does not automatically make a couple suitable to have children/be parents.*

➤ *For a homosexual couple or single parent to have children they must really want the child because of the difficult process they have to go through.*

➤ *Many other sorts of families make very good parents.*

➤ *If God gave scientists the ability to create children for couples then what is wrong with homosexual couples having children?*

➤ *Not against the law.*

➤ *Buddhism does not condemn homosexuality or sex before marriage – it is a loving relationship that is important so having children, if loved, is acceptable.*

➤ *Children enhance any relationship.*
➤ *Many marriages end in divorce and so in this case do not offer the best for children – marriage is no guarantee of stability.*

Hints and tips

You need to make sure you give arguments to agree **and** to disagree with the statement – if you give only one point of view, then you cannot get above half marks.

Your answer must be full of religious content – this is a statement about religious beliefs and teachings.

The top level requires good development of the arguments you present. This means giving the argument and explaining clearly why it supports/contradicts the statement using detailed examples. This level is looking for a lot of development.

Try to get into the habit of offering three for and three against arguments in all your AO2 answers. Explain and provide examples for each, and include teachings if possible – this will help push your response to a higher level.

Theme B: Religion and life

Question 1
Student A

(a) B: new technological developments should all be infinite or long-lasting

ⓔ **Correct.   1 mark**

(b) It causes global warming as the CO_2 damages the ozone layer.

Climate change where the weather patterns are more erratic because of global warming.

ⓔ **Two effects are clearly identified with a little explanation to make the student's understanding clear.   2 marks**

(c) Roman Catholics believe that 'life is sacred' and 'everyone is made in the image of God' so they believe that abortion is wrong. Any life is a creation of God so should be protected not aborted. Even before a child is born, while it is in the womb, at the moment of conception life has begun and therefore cannot be aborted. It is classed as murder and the Bible says 'Do not kill'.

In the Anglican Church they have a different view. They also believe that 'life is sacred' but this would mean the life of the mother too. They don't take the life of the child as being more important than the life of the mother so if her life is in danger by, say, having a serious heart condition then they accept abortion as a necessary evil.

ⓔ **These two beliefs contrast as required, and the student gives developed explanations of them with teachings to explain the religious position.   4 marks**

(d) Religious people should look after the environment because for example in the Bible Christians are given the 'duty of stewardship' by God. This means they have the responsibility to look after all creation for the present times and for future generation. The world is a gift of God's creation, 'everything in it is the Lord's' so we should want to look after it. Also the world is vital for our existence so we should want to look after it. God might punish us if we don't carry out our duty.

Islam says 'the world is green and beautiful' and in order for it to stay that way Muslims must look after it. The 'world is like a mosque' and so as Muslims respect and look after the mosques so they should respect and look after the world. If they worship and respect them, then they hope for a place in paradise and even on Judgement Day if they have 'a tree shoot in their hand, they should make sure it is planted' which shows that even until death looking after the environment is vital for Muslims.

(e) **A very good answer, built on many teachings which clearly answer the question. This student builds from one teaching to the next, thus showing the depth of their religious knowledge.   5 marks**

(e) Hospices are homes for the dying of all ages. When people are diagnosed with an incurable disease that will kill them, when they get near to the end they can chose to die in a hospice. A hospice will care for the pain, relieve as much suffering as possible and care for the relatives of the patient who are probably finding it difficult to cope with the coming loss. They set themselves as an alternative to active euthanasia which is against the law in Britain. The Bible and other holy books say 'do not kill' and that it is God who 'decides on the time to die'. In Islam, Muslims are told about a man who helped a friend to die, and that neither saw paradise. So hospices provide an alternative and they would claim that the work they do negates the need for euthanasia at all. Others might say that even if it is an alternative to active euthanasia it is not an alternative to passive euthanasia. Someone on a life support machine might, if they knew, prefer to be allowed to die or some of those who refuse treatment would like to be able to choose before they get to a certain point. People who have dementia, which is a growing problem, don't want to lose their dignity and not know anyone or not be able to do anything for themselves and so would prefer euthanasia. Hospices do not help in this situation so euthanasia does need to exist.

If an animal is suffering and there is nothing we can do to prevent an agonising death, we do the kindest thing by putting it to sleep. Some use this as an example to show the need to allow euthanasia as an act of kindness. We don't let the animals suffer but with humans we go to the very last point where suffering has already been endured before we give pain relief to such an extent that the person is 'put to sleep' before their last days/hours. This does not seem right so euthanasia is needed. People have often come to terms with their own mortality and want to make a choice, in this case, to die. Some Christians have said that a doctor does not always have the obligation to keep people alive as long as possible so then termination of life should be permitted. Despite hospices being available some still want euthanasia as is shown by those who leave Britain and travel to foreign clinics to be able to die at a time when they choose even though they know this is illegal under British law. Here it is obvious that the availability of a hospice is not a preferred option.

The people who make decisions about whether euthanasia is allowed have obviously not been in a position to experience a choice about euthanasia personally, so perhaps the answer is not that hospices mean there is no need for euthanasia but that there needs to be the choice available for people in such situations. Hospices serve a very important role for the dying but what they provide might not be what all patients want. Someone in that position I believe should have the choice. Religions would have issues with this in terms of sanctity of life but they also have teachings about the quality of life too and it is very difficult to find a balance that everyone is happy with. Both options are needed, although there will always be those who support one or the other. Perhaps until a person is in that position, it is hard to say what the best answer is.

(e) **This is a difficult question and the student writes about it in a very mature way. Teachings are used and there is good depth to the evaluation looking at both sides of each argument. The conclusion is a thoughtful and supported one.   L4: 12 marks**

Question 1

Student B

(a) C: to try and protect an area of nature for the long term

(e) **Incorrect. The correct answer is B: new technological developments should all be infinite or long-lasting. Make sure you understand key terms like these.   0 marks**

(b) Pollution is caused by too much toxic gas in the air and us using our cars too much.

(e) **This student has misunderstood the nature of the question and gives *causes* of pollution rather than its *effects* – what happens as a result of something.   0 marks**

(c) Abortion in Islam is not liked but it does happen. Muslims believe ensoulment takes place at 120 days so abortion can take place before this because the foetus has no soul.

In Judaism they believe the life of the mother, because it actually exists, is the most important and so abortions can take place.

(e) **This answer offers only simple points/explanations without any development. However, it also does not fulfil one of the demands of the question. Answers MUST refer to the 'main religious tradition of Great Britain', by which is meant Christianity or one of its denominations. So this response can only gain 1 mark.   1 mark**

(d) Muslims believe that the world is green and beautiful so they should try and protect it especially as Allah created it all. Allah would judge Muslims well if they stopped any damage.

(e) **This is borderline 1 or 2 marks as the explanation is a little disjointed. It just doesn't explain the ideas/teachings well enough to be 'developed'.   1/2 marks**

Christians should look after the environment because they were given the direct duty of being stewards by God. The Bible says that 'Everything is the Lord's' so even though we live in the world it appears to be on loan to us but still belonging to God – we are here to take care of it for Him. So as Christians that what they should do.

(e) **The second part of this answer is better. The ideas are developed and there are references to teachings.   3/4 marks**

(e) Hospices are homes for the dying that provide pain relief for severe pain so that they can cope until they actually die. At the same time the hospices provide care for the families who are also going through this terrible experience. It is believed by some that if this type of care was developed and was available more widely then this would mean that euthanasia should not be needed.

Others might say that hospices are not the answer for everyone. Hospices exist now but people actually choose to leave the country and travel to clinics that will help them to die so it is obvious that they didn't see a hospice as an answer for them. Also if someone is on a life support machine then a hospice is not the place for them either. There are also some people who have diseases that mean they lose all their memories and can't do anything for themselves and so when diagnosed they would want to have the choice to have a gentle easy death before it all gets too bad for them rather than have to live with no dignity. Hospices are not an answer in this case. Religions generally are against euthanasia because it is God who decides life and death and some believe that He only puts us through the suffering He thinks we can cope with and through prayer he can comfort and support people. However in the name of kindness and compassion many would probably say hospices do a great job for some people but for others euthanasia should be available. The two are needed to provide the best solution for each patient.

(e) **This answer, although weaker than Student A's response, does attempt to look at both sides of what is a very difficult issue. The writing follows and flows but a full conclusion is lacking – the last few lines attempt one.   L3: 7 marks**

Mark scheme

1 (a) 1 mark for the correct answer.

The correct answer is B: new technological developments should all be infinite or long-lasting

Hints and tips

These questions usually rely entirely on knowledge of key words and terms – you need to learn them.

Be careful to read the question carefully as it could ask you what something IS or what it IS NOT.

(b) 1 mark per correct answer, up to 2 marks maximum.

Answers might include:

can damage the air, water and land, creates landfill, more CO_2, global warming, increasing hole in ozone layer, climate change, deforestation, chemical waste in rivers and sea, animals and fish dying, poorer air quality

Hints and tips

Do not explain anything unless instructed to – just give two words or phrases to answer this question. That frees up your time to answer later questions. With this question, answers could include large-scale effects or effects that are more personal or in specific areas.

The language of questions is really important. For this topic, 'types', 'causes', 'reasons', 'effects' and 'consequences' are all words that could be used by the examiner. Make sure you understand what each term is asking for, as if you mix them up you are throwing easy marks away.

(c) Total of 4 marks.

For the first belief given:
- a **simple** explanation of a relevant and accurate point (1 mark)
- a **detailed** explanation of a relevant and accurate point (2 marks)

For the second contrasting belief given:
- a **simple** explanation of a relevant and accurate point (1 mark)
- a **detailed** explanation of a relevant and accurate point (2 marks)

Answers might include:

Roman Catholics *– they believe that abortion is always wrong. They say life is sacred because it was created by God. They also believe that life begins at conception. This means life must be protected from conception, so any abortion is wrong. The Didache states: 'Do not kill your children by abortion.' Vatican II says: 'Life must be protected with the utmost care from the moment of conception.'*

Anglicans *– many accept abortion as a necessary evil. For example, the mother's life may be at risk (e.g. ectopic pregnancy) – her life is also sacred.*

Islam *– abortion is frowned upon. However, for many, ensoulment (when the foetus acquires a soul) only takes place at 120 days. Before this, it may be permissable to have an abortion. For others ensoulment is at 40 days so abortion before this is acceptable. In Islam the life of the mother always takes priority as she already has life, responsibilities and possibly other children.*

Hints and tips

You have to give two **different** beliefs in the answer to this question – writing about one can only get you 2 out of 4 marks.

Always read the whole question including the instructions as this could be vital to prevent a wasted answer.

Answers must include a Christian response – the main religious tradition of Great Britain. To not do so will mean that full marks cannot be gained.

(d) Total of 4 marks + 1 mark

Look for explanation of two different teachings in the answer.

For the first teaching given:
- a **simple** explanation of a teaching which is both clearly relevant to the question and accurate **(1 mark)**
- a **detailed** explanation of a teaching which is both clearly relevant to the question and accurate **(2 marks)**

For the second teaching given:
- a **simple** explanation of a teaching which is both clearly relevant to the question and accurate **(1 mark)**
- a **detailed** explanation of a teaching which is both clearly relevant to the question and accurate **(2 marks)**

Relevant and accurate reference to scripture and/or sacred writing as required. **(1 mark)**

Answers might include:

Christianity – *'The Earth is the Lord's', 'you are stewards of the earth', 'God made the world' 'Respect for life extends to all creation'. Christians expect punishment on Judgement Day for failure to act on the environment. The world is a gift from God which is precious so we should want to look after it for Him. Christians have a responsibility to future generations to be able to live in a clean nd beautiful world.*

Islam – *'The world is green and beautiful', 'the world is a place of worship, 'the world has been created as a mosque', Prophet Muhammad did not waste water, 'when Judgement Day comes a tree shoot in the hand should still be planted'.*

Hints and tips

You have to explain two **different** teachings in the answer to this question.

The mark scheme tells you that the points have to be 'clearly relevant' – if you write something that does not make sense, or that you have to think about to make it relevant, then it is not a good answer.

A good way to answer is to give a teaching, and then explain how it is important.

You do not have to give exact quotations – it is fine to paraphrase. What you have to do is make it obvious that you are referring to something a person definitely said, and that what you say they said is approximately right. This is especially true when you are referring to a long teaching.

Using key technical terms is always very impressive to the examiner. Try to make sure you use them when you can.

(e) These questions are marked according to levels of response – this means your answer is judged for its quality overall, not for how many different arguments you present.

Answers might include:

Arguments in support of the view:

➤ *Hospices help the dying with pain relief so making death easier.*

➤ *Hospices support families to be able to cope with the dying rather than wanting them to die.*

➤ *Hospices mean that people do not have to break the law to show compassion to the dying.*

➤ *If the care is good enough, euthanasia need not be considered.*

➤ *Euthanasia is not supported by most faiths but hospices are.*

➤ *Hospices can relieve physical symptoms, provide emotional and spiritual well-being, support families with patient networks and develop the specific work of the hospices outside to provide better care and to develop new ways of caring for the future – if all this works then euthanasia is not necessary.*

Arguments supporting other views:

➤ *Some people want to die and have control of their own destiny when things get too bad – hospices will not change that.*

➤ *Passive euthanasia still happens even though hospices exist, e.g. someone having a life support machine turned off or refusing treatment.*

➤ *Many religious people, despite religious teachings, believe that in the name of compassion and kindness euthanasia should be available, e.g. where someone has locked-in syndrome.*

➤ *Hospices do not care for all the dying, e.g. people who have mental illness like dementia where they lose their dignity and enjoyment of life. If they had the choice, perhaps they would prefer to die – a hospice would not be the place for them.*

➤ *People travel to other countries to die even with hospices available, so the fact hospices exist clearly does not do away with the perceived need for euthanasia.*

Hints and tips

You need to make sure you give arguments to agree **and** to disagree with the statement – if you give only one point of view, then you cannot get above half marks.

Your answer must be full of religious content – this is a statement about religious beliefs and teachings.

The top level requires good development of the arguments you present. This means giving the argument and explaining clearly why it supports/contradicts the statement using detailed examples. This level is looking for a lot of development.

Try to get into the habit of offering three for and three against arguments in all your AO2 answers. Explain and provide examples for each, and include teachings if possible – this will help push your response to a higher level.

Theme C: The existence of God and revelation

Question 1

Student A

(a) C: science

ⓔ **Correct. Science often finds itself in conflict with religion over the question of God's existence. 1 mark**

(b) They have had personal experience in a vision or have witnessed a miracle.

ⓔ **Two clear ideas are given. 2 marks**

(c) General revelation is when God reveals Himself indirectly or through something. Nature is God's creation and because of this Christians would say we can see God in it. If we look at the work of a painter, we can see clues of themselves in their work, and in the same way God has left clues in His creation. The world looks beautiful, for example mountains, and it shows much design, like a butterfly's wing or spider's web. William Paley tried to prove God exists by using the world and nature as his evidence. We can see His power in the weather, His attention to detail in the planets etc.

An atheist would ask how it can be possible for nature to reveal God as general revelation. First, God does not exist so cannot be revealed and nature is simply nature. To the atheist, religious people are just seeing too much in something because of their beliefs. They want to see God, so they do.

ⓔ **An excellent contrast of ideas, and good use of examples to explain these ideas. 4 marks**

(d) Christians believe in the idea of God as the Trinity. The Apostles Creed says 'I believe in God the Father…. And in Jesus Christ his only son… and the Holy Spirit'. They are three aspects of God each with a different role. The Father is the creator, the Son is God on Earth and the Holy Spirit is what acts in the world now as a guide and support.

Muslims believe in Tawhid – 'He is Allah the One… eternal and absolute…'. God is one – all powerful and all knowing. He is absolute and cannot be split – 'nothing is born of him'. The Qur'an says He (Allah) is eternal and closer to Muslims than their jugular vein. Allah is beyond all human understanding so humans can never completely know Him. Allah has 99 names to express his nature such as the all-merciful and the all-just.

ⓔ **Two developed ideas are given here, both including teachings and with clear explanations of what each chosen religion states about God. 5 marks**

(e) I agree that the argument from miracles proves God exists. First, miracles are breaks in natural law and only God is powerful enough to be able to do this. So if we accept a miracle has happened, then we have to accept that God exists.

Second, miracles are often performed by people we think of as being holy or religious, like Mother Teresa. Clearly these people act on God's behalf and get the power to do the miracles from God. So if they perform miracles, then God must exist.

Third, miracles are always good events. God is all-loving and all-powerful. If a miracle happens where a child has been cured and doctors had said this was impossible, then God must have done this out of love and with his power. So God exists.

Others might disagree with me. First they might say that God doesn't exist so a miracle isn't proving God, it is just an event which was good and which we couldn't explain. We might as well say the miracle fairy did it as saying God did! Second, they might say we can't prove something is a miracle – that is just an interpretation of something. It is especially true if science cannot explain it – that is a case of science not being able to explain because it isn't advanced enough. In time science will explain, so the 'miracle' is really a knowledge gap, not God. Thirdly, someone might say that if we can't prove something was a miracle, then how can something not provable prove God? It is like a lie being used to reinforce a lie!

Overall, I think that miracles do prove God exists as often they are prayed for – miracles answer fervent prayers. Only God can answer prayers and make the impossible possible. However, I recognise this is my belief and so it might not work for someone else

(e) **This is a competent answer clearly presenting each idea, explaining the argument with examples and relating them to the question. It is good to see a conclusion using different ideas than have already been stated. For a high level 4, an evaluation of the ideas is needed – and here each idea is evaluated.   L4: 12 marks**

Question 1
Student B

(a) B: design

(e) **Incorrect. The correct answer is C: science. Make sure you read the question and the key word carefully.   0 marks**

(b) He just does!; He answers prayers.

(e) **The first idea is not a reason but a statement; the second answer is correct.   1 mark**

(c) A humanist like an atheist would say that as there is no such thing as God, it is not possible for something that does not exist to be revealed in any way at all. Nature to be sure is magnificent in the way it works and looks, so we should just look and enjoy the pleasure it gives us. It is not connected to anything… it is just nature!

Christians would disagree as it is God's creation and you can always see a maker in something they have made.

(e) **The first part of this answer is explained and developed though a little more could have been said. The second paragraph hardly satisfies the criteria for a 'simple' explanation as there is little to show the student really understands the point he/she is making in response to the question.   3 marks**

(d) Muslims believe that Allah is both immanent and transcendent. He is 'closer to us than our jugular vein' and listens and answers prayers. He also sends revelations such as the Qur'an through Angel Jibr'il so he is involved in the world. He constantly guides us and knows all our thoughts and actions before we do. He is all-merciful and so we feel close to him in our prayers. God has helped, guided and supported people like Ibrahim and Musa so he must be involved in the world. At the same time He is transcendent. He is not bound by time or space like we are and is eternal. He is beyond all we can ever know and has no limits whereas we do have limits and cannot know him.

(e) **This is a good response and even though it is all from the perspective of one religion it does explain two different beliefs – immanence and transcendence. There is also reference to teachings. However, the part on transcendence could have been developed much further.   4 marks**

(e) Yes, miracles do prove God exists because:
  - Miracles are impossible events – only God can do the impossible.
  - Miracles are always good and people are thankful for them – so this demonstrates God's loving nature is behind them.

  But no, they don't because:
  - What is a miracle? We don't know. So can that prove God?
  - What one person says is a miracle, another disagrees it is – if we can't even get a full agreement, how can we use that to prove God's existence?

  I think miracles don't happen – they are just a label for something science cannot explain yet. So if miracles don't happen, then they can't be used to prove God.

(e) **A bullet list is not the best way to answer an evaluation question but fortunately this response is more than just a list – each point is explained and both sides of the argument are covered. The opinion in the conclusion is logical. Just at level 3.   L3: 7 marks**

Mark scheme

1   (a) 1 mark for the correct answer.
      The correct answer is C: science

Hints and tips

These questions usually rely entirely on knowledge of key words and terms – you need to learn them.

Be careful to read the question carefully as it could ask you what something IS or what it IS NOT.

(b) 1 mark per correct answer, up to 2 marks maximum.
      Answers might include:
      the world is designed and planned so it needs a creator God, God is the first cause because he pre-existed everything, special revelation like visions, miracles, a personal experience and general revelation like holy books and nature, upbringing etc.

Hints and tips

Do not explain anything unless instructed to – just give two words or phrases to answer this question. That frees up your time to answer later questions.

The language of questions is really important. For this topic, 'types', 'causes', 'reasons', 'effects' and 'consequences' are all words that could be used by the examiner. Make sure you understand what each term is asking for, as if you mix them up you are throwing easy marks away.

(c) Total of 4 marks.

For the first belief given:
– for a **simple** explanation of a relevant and accurate point **(1 mark)**
– for a **detailed** explanation of a relevant and accurate point **(2 marks)**

For the second contrasting belief given:
– for a **simple** explanation of a relevant and accurate point **(1 mark)**
– for a **detailed** explanation of a relevant and accurate point **(2 marks)**

Answers might include:

Revelation – *revelation is when God reveals Himself. Nature is seen as a source of revelation by Christians because it is God's creation. Just as an artist leaves clues of themselves in their work, so God had left clues in His creation. That the world looks beautiful – for example, pictures from space; that there seems to be so much design – for example, the seasons, the cycle of nature where plants grow, die, but regrow from seed. William Paley tried to prove God exists by using the world and nature as his evidence of design (behind which there must be a designer, and only God can be that designer). Many Christians believe that in a beautiful sunset, they see God at work, in new life they see God at work – this is nature revealing God.*

Contrasting views:

➤ *An atheist would say that as much as nature might reveal to a believer that there is a God, it reveals nothing to others especially those who believe there is no God or divine being.*

➤ *A humanist would say that as there is no such thing as God, a non-existent being cannot be revealed in any way – nature or otherwise – as there is nothing to be revealed. We should just appreciate the beauty and the patterns.*

➤ *In the Anthropomorphic Principle, we can say that the only reason we ask these questions is because we are able to, it is not a proof that there is a God, rather proof we can think.*

Hints and tips

You have to give two **different** ways in which religious beliefs/teachings influence modern British society in the answer to this question – writing about one way can only get you 2 marks out of 4 marks.

When the question asks you to explain how the religious belief/teaching influences societal attitudes, it is asking for the impact on someone's life – what difference it makes to them and the way they live/behave.

Make sure you provide a non-religious point – the question demands it. Always read the whole question including the instructions as this could be vital to prevent a wasted answer.

(d) Total of 4 marks + 1 mark

Look for explanation of two different teachings in the answer.

For the first teaching given:
– a **simple** explanation of a teaching which is both clearly relevant to the question and accurate **(1 mark)**
– a **detailed** explanation of a teaching which is both clearly relevant to the question and accurate **(2 marks)**

For the second teaching given:
– a **simple** explanation of a teaching which is both clearly relevant to the question and accurate **(1 mark)**
– a **detailed** explanation of a teaching which is both clearly relevant to the question and accurate **(2 marks)**

Relevant and accurate reference to scripture and/or sacred writing as required. **(1 mark)**

Answers might include:
Christianity – *One God, Trinity (Father, Son, Holy Spirit), eternal, transcendent, immanent, creator, judge/just, all-powerful, all-knowing, benevolent etc.*
Islam – *Tawhid (Oneness of God), 99 names, judge, all-powerful, all-knowing, all-merciful/just/compassionate/knowing/etc., creator.*

Hints and tips

You have to explain two **different** teachings in the answer to this question.

The mark scheme tells you that the points have to be 'clearly relevant' – if you read (or write) something that does not make sense, or that you have to think about to make it relevant, then it is not a good answer.

A good way to answer is to give a teaching, and then explain how it is important.

You do not have to give exact quotations – it is fine to paraphrase. What you have to do is make it obvious that you are referring to something a person definitely said, and that what you say they said is approximately right. This is especially true when you are referring to a long teaching.

Using key technical terms is always very impressive to the examiner. Try to make sure you use them when you can.

(e) These questions are marked according to levels of response – this means your answer is judged for its quality overall, not for how many different arguments you present.

Answers might include:

Arguments in support of view:

➤ *Miracles are impossible events and simply do not happen – but God can do anything even the impossible so he must exist because miracles do.*
➤ *Miraculous events are always good happenings and they therefore reveal the loving nature of God.*
➤ Miracles are breaks in natural law and this is only possible for God.
➤ *Miracles have a religious connection – performed by religious people so they can do this because God gives them that power – Jesus, Mother Teresa, Roman Catholic saints.*
➤ *Holy books all describe miracles, historically miracles have been 'proven', so this shows God has been involved in His creation throughout time.*

Arguments supporting other views:

➤ *If a miracle is an unexplained event how can this then explain God's existence?*
➤ *Events can be interpreted by different people in different ways.*
➤ *Miracles are events that science cannot explain right now but that does not mean they won't be explained in the future – it is just a matter of waiting for science to work it out.*
➤ *How can an unprovable event prove an unprovable God? – this makes no sense.*

Hints and tips

You need to make sure you give arguments to agree **and** to disagree with the statement – if you give only one point of view, then you cannot get above half marks.

Your answer must be full of religious content – this is a statement about religious beliefs and teachings.

The top level requires good development of the arguments you present. This means giving the argument and explaining clearly why it supports/contradicts the statement using detailed examples. This level is looking for a lot of development.

Try to get into the habit of offering three for and three against arguments in all your AO2 answers. Explain and provide examples for each, and include teachings if possible – this will help push your response to a higher level.

If time is limited as the exam comes to an end, the method of listing as in Student B's response is a way of getting as many ideas down as possible in a limited amount of time and will be given credit. Do not use bullet points if there is no time issue as it does not look impressive.

Theme D: Religion, peace and conflict

Question 1

Student A

(a) A: not to blame someone any more for the wrongs they have done

(e) Correct. Forgiveness is a religious idea to allow the removing of blame so that people can move on with their lives.   1 mark

(b) War creates victims (like injured soldiers); many deaths.

(e) Two correctly identified ideas.   2 marks

(c) The Quaker Society is non-violent. They refuse to participate in any forms of violence – even as soldiers in times of war. They have an absolute morality on this topic so a decision cannot be made depending on the circumstances. They claim the 'Spirit of Christ, leads us in Truth, and so will never move us to fight'. There is something of God in every person and if we can focus on this then through negotiation and forgiveness and understanding, situations can be resolved better than by turning to violence.

Other Christian groups would argue more for a relative morality that violence can be used in certain cases. They agree with the Just War idea, and as a last resort or as a necessary evil, or in self-defence, violence in a war sense can be used. They also condemn all other forms of violence like domestic or sexual violence.

(e) This response shows two developed, contrasting views. The student explains both positions clearly.   4 marks

(d) Terrorism is acts of violence that create fear and target civilians in their daily lives, which is why they are unlawful and seen as murderous acts. Christians believe that they should love their enemies and that God rewards the peacemakers so terrorism is totally against this. It kills innocent people deliberately, often in mass killings, and is the wrong way to achieve what the terrorists want.

Islam believes that acts of terrorism are wrong and there is no justification for it in Islamic teaching or texts. People who carry out terrorism make others live in fear and actual terrorist acts kill innocent people, which is never right. The Qur'an says 'do not kill each other, for God is merciful to you. If any of you does these things, out of hostility and injustice we shall make him suffer fire' (Qur'an), which suggests punishment in the afterlife for such acts.

(e) **A mature answer, excellently constructed. The student uses religious teachings to explain each religion's stance on terrorism.   5 marks**

(e) Pacifism is the belief that war and violence are always wrong and therefore it is not a matter of consideration of circumstances but rather there is no debate, it should never happen. Pacifists feel that there is nothing to be gained by war and that it simply makes the situation worse. This would be supported by certain religious teachings like 'Those who live by the sword, die by the sword' showing that violence gains nothing. Quakers for example believe that they are totally adhering to their faith by being pacifists. Islam means peace and the only way of truly ensuring peace is to be a pacifist. There are plenty of teachings across all religions that would agree with the statement. If we look through history, it is clear that war gains little, many people die, lives are ruined and peace is hardly ever created so there must be better ways to sort out these serious situations. It is often said that religious people should set good examples for the rest of society, so if religious people in the military refused to fight and others followed their lead there would be no war as politicians are not going to fight and so other ways to peace would have to be found. Pacifists are not cowards, they simply believe there are better ways, and as religious people if they truly follow the teachings and example of many religious founders and leaders then perhaps all religious people should be pacifists.

However, the question has a very definite angle to it by saying 'everyone who is religious' should be a pacifist. If this was actually true there would surely be a specific teaching or commandment saying so. If we look at wars that have taken place like the Second World War, war was a last resort. Hitler acted against promises he made and so war was the only option. Religious people do not go into war lightly, but sometimes it is a necessary evil. Europe could not let Hitler just wage war, kill people and occupy countries – something had to be done. This has been the case in many wars. Most political leaders do not send their armies into battle easily but sometimes decisions have to be made for the common good. Most religions suggest that where necessary war can be fought – for protection of people and self-defence for example – and so it has to be an option. This is why we have the Just War theory to try to ensure that even where war is fought, there are rules that sides should follow to ensure a justified cause, lessen the impact and bring it to an end as soon as is possible. There are people who abuse this, like terrorists or undemocratic leaders, but they would do even more harm if they knew all religious people were pacifists.

In conclusion, in an ideal world I believe the statement should be true but in the modern world this may not be possible. There has to be the threat of war even if it is not taken up. War should be a last resort in the ideal world too and sometimes it is and sometimes it isn't. If the world could work to all being pacifists everyone would benefit, but history tell us this is perhaps not possible.

(e) **This is an excellent response which develops each point made, evaluates it and uses religious teachings to support the different views. The conclusion shows that the student understands the arguments on both sides.   L4: 12 marks**

Question 1

Student B

(a) B: to forget a wrong action done to a person

e **Incorrect. The correct answer is A: not to blame someone any more for the wrongs they have done. Make sure you understand the key terms, and always read the question and all the options carefully.   0 marks**

(b) Civil and nuclear

e **These are types of war, not its consequences.   0 marks**

(c) Violence is about using actions that threaten or actually harm others and within Islam this cannot be justified. In practice violence involving Muslims has broken out in protests and in conflicts between religious groups but this does not reflect teachings. Muslims are told 'do not take life which God has made sacred' and any act of violence puts life at risk so cannot be right.

Christians will accept violence as in war if it is in self-defence.

e **A good developed response in the first paragraph, so 2 marks here. The second paragraph, although correct as a statement of fact, needs more evidence of the student's understanding of the position of the main religious tradition of Great Britain (Christian) on violence. As it stands it does not qualify as a 'simple explanation'.   2 marks**

(d) Some Muslims say that terrorism is acceptable because of the cause they are fighting for, but actually the Qur'an states that to take another man's life is the greatest sin and this must be even more true if innocent lives are being taken.

Christians are told 'Do not kill' and as terrorism is mass killing it has to be wrong, so Christians disagree with it.

e **Neither of the two correct ideas in this response is sufficiently developed to show the student's full understanding of the effect of each religion's position. The two teachings are correct and simply applied.   3 marks**

(e) Most religious teachings are about peace like in the Bible where Jesus says the peacemakers will be blessed so that would seem to tell Christians to be pacifists, although also in the Bible it does talk about wars, especially in the Old Testament. Jesus and his supporters could have started a war because his country was occupied by the Romans but he chose not to, and when his disciple cut off the man's ear Jesus was angry with him and told him not to retaliate and that no one wins if we use violence against violence. Also people are told to love their neighbour and that can't be happening if we are at war. Jesus tells us also to 'treat others the way we wish to be treated' and again we wouldn't want war so why go to war somewhere else. All these teachings tell me that certainly for Christians we should all be pacifists.

Many Muslims would also say the same thing because the name of their religion actually means 'peace' and the only way to do this is to be a pacifist. Peace is about respect, reconciliation and forgiveness not about revenge or retaliation. Allah tells us 'Do not take life, which God has made sacred' and in any war soldiers and innocent civilians get killed so in no way can it be right. Many Muslims many believe pacifism is a good position to have. Others say you have to fight if necessary.

(e) This is a fair answer with lots of points made and teachings used. However, what is written does not cover both sides of the question or different views, so it is limited to L2 only (the last sentence is not enough for a 'different point of view). It is quite common for examiners to see answers that do not cover different sides or where 'agrees' and disagrees' are mixed up, so always re-read an answer to check you have done what the question requires you to. Some good examples offered but the evaluation is a little simplistic.   **L2: 6 marks**

Mark scheme

1   **(a)** 1 mark for the correct answer.

The correct answer is A: not to blame someone any more for the wrongs they have done

Hints and tips

These questions usually rely entirely on knowledge of key words and terms – you need to learn them.

Be careful to read the question carefully as it could ask you what something IS or what it IS NOT.

(b) 1 per correct answer, up to 2 marks maximum.

Answers might include:

death (both civilian and military), destruction of land, homes, buildings and communities, famine, disease, loss, hate, land expansion, change in power balance, peace

Hints and tips

Do not explain anything unless instructed to – just give two words or phrases to answer this question. That frees up your time to answer later questions.

The language of questions is really important. For this topic, 'types', 'causes', 'reasons', 'effects' and 'consequences' are all words that could be used by the examiner. Make sure you understand what each term is asking for, as if you mix them up you are throwing easy marks away.

(c) Total of 4 marks.

For the first belief given:
  – a **simple** explanation of a relevant and accurate point   **(1 mark)**.
  – a **detailed** explanation of a relevant and accurate point   **(2 marks)**.

For the second contrasting belief given:
  – a **simple** explanation of a relevant and accurate point   **(1 mark)**
  – a **detailed** explanation of a relevant and accurate point   **(2 marks)**

Answers might include:

*While **Christianity** follows Jesus' teachings of peace, there are those within the religion who will see it as acceptable in given situations. The Catholic, Orthodox and Anglican denominations accept the Just War theory, which provides conditions within which war may be fought. Certain groups believe it is acceptable to chastise children physically ('Whoever spares the rod hates their children, but the one who loves their children is careful to discipline them' Proverbs 13:24). Most Christians would accept the use of violence* *in self-defence. Some Christians agree with the use of the death penalty – in spite of it being the ultimate violence inflicted on a person – out of a sense of abhorrence for what that criminal has done.*

The **Quaker Society** *is non-violent. Quakers refuse to participate in any forms of violence – even as soldiers in times of war. They will carry 'no outward weapon'. They claim the 'Spirit of Christ, which leads us in Truth, will never move us to fight'. There is something of God in every person, and appealing to that can resolve issues better than violence can.*

The **Catholic Church's** *stance is that there is dignity to being human, and to inflict violence on them, or to receive it, is a denial of that dignity. Pope Francis has spoken out against the death penalty. Pope Benedict XVI spoke out against sexual violence as a grave sin.*

Islam *suggests that if someone comes in peace to them, they should come in peace too. However, violence can also be justified to rectify injustices especially against fellow Muslims – there is no absolute right to use violence.*

Hints and tips

You have to give two **different** beliefs in the answer to this question – writing about one can only get you 2 out of 4 marks.

Always read the whole question including the instructions as this could be vital to prevent a wasted answer.

(d) Total of 4 marks + 1 mark

Look for explanation of two different teachings in the answer.

For the first teaching given:
– a **simple** explanation of a teaching which is both clearly relevant to the question and accurate **(1 mark)**
– a **detailed** explanation of a teaching which is both clearly relevant to the question and accurate **(2 marks)**

For the second teaching given:
– a **simple** explanation of a teaching which is both clearly relevant to the question and accurate **(1 mark)**
– a **detailed** explanation of a teaching which is both clearly relevant to the question and accurate **(2 marks)**

Relevant and accurate reference to scripture and/or sacred writing as required. **(1 mark)**

Answers might include:

Terrorism makes people live in fear so all religions disagree with it. It often involves mass killing of many innocent people and is therefore against all religious teachings.

Christianity *follows 'Do not kill', love your enemies, blessed are the peacemakers.*

Islam *means peace, 'the greatest sin is to take another's life', 'do not kill each other, for God is merciful to you. If any of you does these things, out of hostility and injustice we shall make him suffer fire' (Qur'an).*

Most religions accept that there might be a time to fight but terrorism is not acceptable, it is not proportionate, targeted, its direct purpose is to kill as many as possible, suicide is wrong, it attacks people's freedoms and democratic rights.

Hints and tips

You have to explain two **different** teachings in the answer to this question.

The mark scheme tells you that the points have to be 'clearly relevant' – if you write something that does not make sense, or that you have to think about to make it relevant, then it is not a good answer.

A good way to answer is to give a teaching, and then explain how it is important.

You do not have to give exact quotations – it is fine to paraphrase. What you have to do is make it obvious that you are referring to something a person definitely said, and that what you say they said is approximately right. This is especially true when you are referring to a long teaching.

Using key technical terms is always very impressive to the examiner. Try to make sure you use them when you can.

(e) These questions are marked according to levels of response – this means your answer is judged for its quality overall, not for how many different arguments you present.

Answers might include:

Arguments in support of the view:

➤ *The majority of religious teaching preaches peace not war.*
➤ *The Commandments tell people 'Do not kill', Islam says all life 'God has made sacred'.*
➤ *Christians would say that they are truly following their faith if they are pacifists.*
➤ *Pacifism is believed by some to be more powerful than war.*
➤ *If all soldiers refused to fight then there would be no war and other solutions would have to be found.*
➤ *All religions teach about treating others and respecting others as you would want to be treated – no one wants to be killed so why kill others in war?*

Arguments supporting other views:

➤ *Most religious holy books allow the take up of arms as a last resort, or in self-defence.*
➤ *A country simply cannot sit back and allow anyone to attack as it needs to protect itself and its people.*
➤ *Sometimes war is a necessary evil for the greater good.*
➤ *Sometimes war is needed to create peace and no other method is appropriate.*
➤ *Each situation needs to be assessed on merit rather than having a definitive view.*

Hints and tips

You need to make sure you give arguments to agree **and** to disagree with the statement – if you give only one point of view, then you cannot get above half marks.

Your answer must be full of religious content – this is a statement about religious beliefs and teachings.

The top level requires good development of the arguments you present. This means giving the argument and explaining clearly why it supports/contradicts the statement using detailed examples. This level is looking for a lot of development.

Try to get into the habit of offering three for and three against arguments in all your AO2 answers. Explain and provide examples for each, and include teachings if possible – this will help push your response to a higher level.

Theme E: Religion, crime and punishment

Question 1

Student A

(a) B: to make the punishment fit the crime so it almost seems like an act of revenge

(e) **Correct. An example of retribution is 'a life for a life' – the punishment is equal to the crime (in as much as that is possible).   1 mark**

(b) Emotional support to get over the crimes and help for young victims.

(e) **Two correct, clear answers.   2 marks**

(c) In Islamic Law they allow the use of corporal or physical punishment. They use beatings or lashes like 100 for men caught in adultery and cutting hands off for stealing. The point is to act as a deterrent to the criminal and others who see these punishments, as often for example the beatings are done in public. The Qur'an says how these punishments should be done.

In Christianity, the Quakers especially campaigned to have corporal punishment removed from law as they see it as barbaric. It is cruel and does no good as treating criminals violently will not reform them but make them worse. It is too much like revenge than reform, which is a Christian's main aim of punishment.

(e) **The two detailed answers here are well explained and clearly written.   4 marks**

(d) In the Bible Paul tells the early Christian communities that they should follow the law – 'Obey the laws of the land' and that the laws and rulers are 'instituted by God'. Therefore the law should be followed. Christians see this to mean that they follow the laws that are just and show opposition to those that are not because God would not institute unjust laws. When people do not follow the law they should expect to be punished.

The Qur'an provides Shari'ah Law, which is the law of Allah, and they must believe that this is the only true law on earth. However, they are to follow the laws of the land that they reside in – 'Fulfil your obligations', and to try and promote Shari'ah Law. These laws are strict and punishments follow as any civil law broken means religious law has also been broken because the two are the same thing. Some Muslims believe world law will never be just until the entire world follows Shari'ah.

(e) **This is an excellent answer. The student makes good use of teachings along with developed explanations.   5 marks**

(e) Prison is a place away from society where criminals are watched and controlled so that the public feel safe. It is for dangerous people and it could well be argued that anyone who commits any kind of crime could be said to be dangerous and so locking them up is the best form of punishment. None of us like being victims of crime, even the most minor, and when this happen to us it is a massive issue. If a person is put in prison then we feel safer. Others might disagree saying there are dangerous and not so dangerous people, and only the ones that threaten our lives in a major way should be locked up, and there needs to be a hierarchy of punishments rather than being hard line from the start. Religious people believe in reform and second chances, and prison just would not reform certain people.

Prison also allows all the aims of punishment to be achieved: society is protected; the criminals are worked with to allow reform; justice is done so retribution is apparent, and the idea of prison would deter many. Others might say that many are not reformed, but made worse with the experience. It hardens them and makes them more full of hate, and we must remember many people in prison are damaged before they go in because of their lives so far.

Many religions like Islam would probably agree with this, as Islamic law punishments are harsh so they act as a deterrent and therefore protect people as opposed to softer punishments like community service. Christians would agree to a certain extent with the statement but want more of a balance dependent upon the crime. Christians have worked for many years for prison reform, which suggests that prison conditions and life need to be far better than they are at the moment, especially if all criminals are to be sent there. Also it would be totally unmanageable, far too many people to lock up. However, others might suggest that it could cut down on minor crime because of the threat of a harsh punishment. Prison is not always the best way to reform, which is the ultimate aim of any punishment. Time spent in prison disrupts the lives of the criminal, the families, their jobs and this can all make a situation worse. People learn in different ways and a judge needs to have a variety of punishments to be able to use for the system to try and do its best for a very wide range of people. To put every criminal in prison almost feels like taking revenge, when compensation and forgiveness could be a far better solution.

In conclusion, I do not feel that prison is the best way for all criminals, apart from those like murderers who we have to lock up. I feel that the evidence suggests that prison does not have a positive impact on very many. In other words, it does not reform and so if we then send everyone there how will this help? There would have to be a massive shake up of prisons if they were to be used for everyone. Also there are far more appropriate punishments used that do work and have the desired outcomes. Many religious people might also suggest that instead of looking at the punishments perhaps we need to look at preventing crimes in the first place, and that this is more the answer. We need to spread a message of respect, compassion and help to create a better society/community so punishments would not be needed. If we follow 'Love your neighbour' or 'treat others as you wish to be treated' like Christians should – this is the real answer as crimes would not happen.

(e) **A good response, particularly because it is not easy to put religious ideas/teachings into such a secular question, but this student has succeeded. The argument on both sides is very well evaluated.   L4: 12 marks**

Question 1
Student B

(a)   C: to make up for the crime that was committed – to repair the damage

(e)   **Incorrect. The correct answer is B: to make the punishment fit the crime so it almost seems like an act of revenge. These questions usually rely entirely on knowledge of key words and terms – you need to learn them.   0 marks**

(b)   Support and help.

(e)   **These ideas are too vague and simply repeat two words found in the question.   0 marks**

(c)   Christians see corporal punishment as just cruel and not what the law should be doing because using violence is always wrong. Often criminals have had bad lives already so this won't help. Muslims allow hands to be cut off though and beatings as well for criminals. It is a tough punishment to put people off.

(e) **The first idea about Christian belief is correct but is only marked as a simple explanation; it would need more – such as the last sentence being explained – to achieve 2 marks for a detailed explanation. The second idea about Muslim belief is again correct but short of explanation in the same way.   2 marks**

(d) Christians are told they should follow the law because they should be good role models in society. If they are breaking the law they don't 'love their neighbours' because there is always a victim of crime.

In the Bible it says to 'treat others as you wish to be treated' and no one wants to be a victim of crime so why make other people victims? You don't want your house broken into, or family members killed so why do it to other people? Therefore Christians must follow the law so that everyone is safe.

(e) **This is not really the ideal answer because it does not talk about what Christians or other religions believe about following the law of the land. However, although Student B may not know any religious references to following laws he/she does use the teachings he/she knows know as relevantly as possible.**

These two teachings can be used for many answers and while not ideal here, they are nevertheless correct. The first paragraph is only a simple explanation for 1 mark, but the second would pick up the 2 marks for a developed explanation. 1 mark for the reference to relevant teachings.   4 marks

(e) I think there are two key parts to this question, first whether prison is better than other forms of punishment, and second whether this is true for all criminals. Prison is only one form of punishment in the UK, and how do we assess whether it is the best form? For some, prison will work, for others it won't and we see this with the number of reoffenders, and at the same time for example tagging or community service works for some but not others. The word 'better' implies successful and this is hard to determine. Christians would say better in terms of 'are they reformed?' but Muslims might ask 'has prison deterred them from further crimes?' so it is a difficult question.

Prison I believe is better for certain criminals like killers or rapists as they have to be locked up because they are dangerous. However, for minor crimes it seems like it is too harsh. Surely we need different levels of punishments for different crimes? Also reasons behind the crimes can have a massive impact on the punishment. Even for murderers – is a woman killing her abusive husband the same as a man killing another person in cold blood? Also some crimes don't deserve prison.

How we treat criminals is one of society's unanswerable questions really. We have been doing it for centuries but nothing stops everyone and this is why I believe that we need a range of punishments and in each case to try to find the one that is most suitable and the one that hopefully will have the best outcomes. Christians want to see justice served but also we do have a responsibility for the criminal too and prison could make things worse. Perhaps we need to spend more time on crime prevention, and if we lived more according to religious principles then the need for punishment would not be there.

(e) **This is a good answer, but it is written from a totally different angle than that of Student A. It also shows how hard it is to include religious ideas in such a secular question but there is some attempt at this. Both sides of the argument are included with evaluation attempted.   L3: 8/9 marks**

Mark scheme

1   **(a)** 1 mark for the correct answer.

      The correct answer is B: to make the punishment fit the crime so it almost seems like an act of revenge.

Hints and tips

These questions usually rely entirely on knowledge of key words and terms – you need to learn them.

Be careful to read the question carefully as it could ask you what something IS or what it IS NOT.

  (b) 1 mark per correct answer, up to 2 marks maximum.

     Answers might include:

     emotional and practical support, practical tips to keep safe, specific support in cases of rape or abuse, help for young victims, help with communication for foreign language speakers, advice about dealing with any crime, putting people in touch with legal services if required

Hints and tips

Do not explain anything unless instructed to – just give two words or phrases to answer this question. That frees up your time to answer later questions.

Do not simply repeat the words in the question in lower-mark questions, especially those asking for definitions and causes.

  (c) Total of 4 marks.

     For the first belief given:

      – a **simple** explanation of a relevant and accurate point   **(1 mark)**

      – a **detailed** explanation of a relevant and accurate point   **(2 marks)**

     For the second contrasting belief given:

      – a **simple** explanation of a relevant and accurate point   **(1 mark)**

      – a **detailed** explanation of a relevant and accurate point   **(2 marks)**

     Answers might include:

     Christianity *– as a rule does not support the use of corporal punishment. Many point to the idea of human dignity, and that this kind of punishment goes against that. As a form of violence, corporal punishment is seen as wrong by many as that is not merciful, but more like taking revenge. The belief that violence leads to violence means that criminals dealt with in this way will not be reformed. Christian groups such as the Quakers worked to reform this kind of punishment in UK law.*

     Islamic (Shari'ah) Law *– includes the legitimate use of corporal punishment. The Qur'an states that it must be proportionate, necessary and carried out publicly (24:2). Methods sanctioned by the Qur'an include beatings/lashes, and amputation (5:38). It is a punishment and deterrent.*

Hints and tips

You have to give two **different** beliefs in the answer to this question – writing about one can only get you 2 out of 4 marks.

Always read the whole question including the instructions as this could be vital to prevent a wasted answer.

(d) Total of 4 marks + 1 mark

Look for explanation of two different teachings in the answer.

For the first teaching given:
- a **simple** explanation of a teaching which is both clearly relevant to the question and accurate **(1 mark)**
- a **detailed** explanation of a teaching which is both clearly relevant to the question and accurate **(2 marks)**

For the second teaching given:
- a **simple** explanation of a teaching which is both clearly relevant to the question and accurate **(1 mark)**
- a **detailed** explanation of a teaching which is both clearly relevant to the question and accurate **(2 marks)**

Relevant and accurate reference to scripture and/or sacred writing as required. **(1 mark)**

Answers might include:

Christianity *– Christians believe the law has a responsibility to punish and care for the criminal whilst trying to reform them. It also has concern for their reform so that they can be released back into society. Therefore, there can be conflict between severe punishments and the Christian belief in help, love and reform. Some Christians want more of an emphasis on 'justice' based on the 'an eye for an eye' teaching from the Bible. St Paul told people to 'obey the laws of the land' and Jesus told people to pay their taxes as the law states. Also St Paul states that leaders are instituted by God so we should follow their laws.*

Islam *– Muslims believe that a person should obey the laws of a country that they live in and fight to change the law if unjust. Many think Shari'ah Law is the only law as this comes from Allah. The legal system in Muslim countries is based on Shari'ah Law so the laws of the land are the laws of God. True justice can only be served on earth when Allah's law is in place.*

Hints and tips

You have to explain two **different** teachings in the answer to this question.

The mark scheme tells you that the points have to be 'clearly relevant' – if you write something that does not make sense, or that you have to think about to make it relevant, then it is not a good answer.

A good way to answer is to give a teaching, and then explain how it is important.

You do not have to give exact quotations – it is fine to paraphrase. What you have to do is make it obvious that you are referring to something a person definitely said, and that what you say they said is approximately right. This is especially true when you are referring to a long teaching.

Using key technical terms is always very impressive to the examiner. Try to make sure you use them when you can.

(e) These questions are marked according to levels of response – this means your answer is judged for its quality overall, not for how many different arguments you present.

Answers might include:

Arguments in support of the view:

➤ *Prison is a harsh punishment which many learn from and do not go on to reoffend whereas softer punishments do not often deter criminals.*

➤ *Prison is a time for offenders to reflect, see the error of what they have done and move on, reformed.*

➤ *Prison allows all the aims of punishment to be fulfilled.*

➤ *Prison is better than the death penalty as criminals have to live with what they have done.*

➤ *All criminals are 'dangerous' in one way or another and prison protects society.*

Arguments supporting other views:

➤ *All criminals cannot go to prison as there simply are not enough places.*

➤ *Prison is not suitable for minor criminals.*

➤ *Prison could make minor criminals worse if they mix with hardened criminals.*

➤ *Many prisoners reoffend so this shows that prison does not work.*

➤ *Unless dangerous to society do all criminals need to be sent to prison?*

➤ *Too expensive for the benefits gained.*

➤ *To be locked up could be detrimental to family, future job and morale.*

➤ *Cannot put young people in prison.*

➤ *Prison is not always the best way to reform and so religious people would not support this view.*

➤ *There has to be a variety and hierarchical structure to deal with different crimes.*

➤ *Community service or a fine might be the better, more positive, option for some criminals.*

➤ *The death penalty is seen as better than prison for the worst criminals.*

Hints and tips

You need to make sure you give arguments to agree **and** to disagree with the statement – if you give only one point of view, then you cannot get above half marks.

Your answer must be full of religious content – this is a statement about religious beliefs and teachings.

The top level requires good development of the arguments you present. This means giving the argument and explaining clearly why it supports/contradicts the statement using detailed examples. This level is looking for a lot of development.

Try to get into the habit of offering three for and three against arguments in all your AO2 answers. Explain and provide examples for each, and include teachings if possible – this will help push your response to a higher level.

Theme F: Religion, human rights and social justice

Question 1

Student A

(a) A: Salvation Army

ⓔ Correct. **1 mark**

(b) Upbringing and the media.

ⓔ Two clear reasons. **2 marks**

(c) Christians believe that God created us all equal and free. The creation story says everyone was created in the image of God and as such gives us freedom. Dignitas Personae says that a human has a right to religious freedom. Jesus in his teachings tried to win over people by the power of his argument. Jesus allowed them to make up their own minds to believe as they wished. In Britain, people can choose what to believe or what not to believe in without any fear from others.

In Islam it is different. They believe everyone is born a Muslim but many choose the wrong path. They consider Buddhism and Sikhism as not acceptable and Hindus as even less so because they worship many Gods. It is fine to be a Christian or Jew (Muhammad allowed Jews to practise religion in Madinah) because both are 'people of the book' but if anyone leaves Islam in a Muslim country they can be put to death. So there is no real religious freedom.

(e) **The student gives two good contrasting religious ideas here, both clearly developed. 4 marks**

(d) Christianity teaches 'there is neither Jew nor Gentile, slave or free man, male or female. We are all equal in Christ' clearly indicating that people should not be separated for any reason. Christ unites us all and in the case of the question, people of all races and colours should be equal.

Muslims are told that 'everyone is as equal as the teeth on a comb' because 'Allah created everyone equal but different in design'. If racism occurs then this would be an act not only negative to the person/group concerned but seemingly criticising Allah's design to make us all different. Muslims can never know better than Allah Himself so racism should never be an issue.

(e) **This student gives two good ideas which are both developed by providing the religious teaching and explaining how it should be understood in practice.   5 marks**

(e) Statistics show that over half the world's people still live in poverty and for religious people this is a great concern. Christians and Muslims and other religions, for example in the Bible/Qur'an/and other holy books, are given the duty of stewardship by God, and with the extent of the poverty issue it appears religious people are failing in their duty to God and there can be no greater concern for them. Many religious teachings tell people that they aren't religious, or not showing enough compassion or not even loving God when others go hungry or are in poverty, so the poverty issue is so severe it does impact directly on religious people's lives. For religious people in the modern world there are also modern issues like people trafficking and excessive loans which are showing how poverty and desperate need are being exploited for money, which again goes against all religious teachings. Religious people have always contributed to trying to end poverty, but the problem just seems to get worse and is more unanswerable now than at any point in history so it is the greatest problem. Jesus himself fed 5,000 people from very little yet today there is massive food overflow and still people are starving in poverty.

Others might say that poverty is not the problem, it is the causes of it that are the issue such as environmental damage causing floods, famine and disease, war, greed and power, and if we solve these, then poverty will be massively reduced. Poverty is just the result of human evil one way or another or at least selfishness. In terms of stewardship, it is not just poverty that is the problem for this duty but far greater issues like the destruction of the whole planet and our irresponsible actions towards others that need to be focused on. Also many people in the world aren't affected by poverty at all so it is not an issue for them whereas other issues might well be. It may be an issue when we are forced to think about it by the media or charities but most of the time it never crosses our minds. Over history great effort has been made to solve the poverty issue and no improvements are seen, so many stop bothering and focus on things that can be solved or helped.

For religious people there are many issues in the world that in an ideal world would not be happening. If people practised more of what religion tells them too we would live in a far better world for everyone. However, there is no doubt poverty is a major concern, but there are many concerns in competition to be the greatest. It is probably the greatest travesty because in reality it shouldn't be happening in a modern world with the riches that exist. It is probably better to look at it, thinking more about how it can be solved, rather than focus on whether it's the greatest problem or not. Hopefully then religious people can put their teachings into action to see progress being made.

ⓔ **This might seem like a straightforward question but achieving the higher mark levels requires careful focus on the attitudes of 'religious people'. The ideas discussed could end up being very secular but this student has done a good job of concenrtrating on religious attitudes. It would not be awarded full marks, but it is an excellent attempt.   L4: 11 marks**

Question 1
Student B

(a) B: Shelter

ⓔ **Incorrect. The correct answer is A: Salvation Army. Shelter is not a religious charity. Make sure you read the question carefully.   0 marks**

(b) They don't like people of a different colour and they are prejudiced because they learnt it from their parents.

ⓔ **The second reason is fine as an answer (upbringing) but the first is not a reason – *why* don't they like people of a different colour?   1 mark**

(c) Many Christians believe that the only way to salvation is through Jesus Christ and so they actively go out and try to convert people to Christianity. Some believe that as long as people lead a good moral life then they can still enter heaven so this allows them to see that other faiths are acceptable.

ⓔ **This is a good response as far as it goes and accesses the 2 marks for a detailed explanation of one belief. Failure to include a second, contrasting belief means this student loses the further 2 marks available.   2 marks**

(d) Christians would say that racism is wrong because God loves the fair minded. Being racist is not fair because it is a judgement that is made without any real evidence.

Islam believes that racism is wrong because Muhammad (pbuh) set the example by allowing a black African visitor to Madinah to carry out the call to prayer. He was criticised for this by the community, presumably because the man was 'black'. Muhammad's response was to ask if the man was a Muslim. This means that Muslims can be of all colours and therefore have the same rights as each other.

ⓔ **The teaching in the first paragraph is from the wrong religion – it is Islamic not Christian so the answer is confused. The development of the idea is not enough to gain the marks for a simple explanation. The second paragraph is a developed answer, including correct teachings and a good example.   3 marks**

(e) Poverty is the greatest problem in the world today because we only have to look at how many people live in it and die because of it. Also we can look at the massive amount of money and time that have gone into solving it, yet it seems like little progress is being made. This clearly shows it is the greatest problem because we can't solve it.

In the world today we see rich people getting richer and poor people getting poorer. Some people have no food and water yet others are developing space exploration for example. This cannot be right, but poverty has been with us so long we have come to accept it or more accept the fact that the problem is too big for us to deal with anymore. At the same time it gets worse with things like the migrant crisis and people trafficking for which there are few answers.

Some would say there are greater problems like war, the threat of nuclear war, or a terrorist attack in the world today and it seems more important that people die in a Paris terrorist attack or while on holiday in Turkey than the thousands who die daily in Africa because of poverty. This shows it has been overtaken as a key concern for people today.

(e) **This answer presents some good arguments, but the 'agree' side is by far the stronger making the argument one-sided. The student needs to give more ideas on each side of the argument. There is no reference to religion at all, which is the main downfall of the answer (even though some of the ideas may well be held by religious people). There is also no conclusion. Therefore a mark just at the top of L2/bottom L3 would be appropriate.   L2/3: 6 marks/7 marks**

Mark scheme

1   **(a)** 1 mark for the correct answer.

The correct answer is A: Salvation Army

Hints and tips

These questions usually rely entirely on knowledge of key words and terms – you need to learn them.

Be careful to read the question carefully as it could ask you what something IS or what it IS NOT.

(b) 1 mark per correct answer, up to 2 marks maximum.

Answers might include:

upbringing, media, fear and ignorance, personal experience, scapegoating

Hints and tips

Do not explain anything unless instructed to – just give two words or phrases to answer this question. That frees up your time to answer later questions.

Do not simply repeat the words in the question in lower-mark questions, especially those asking for definitions and causes.

(c) Total of 4 marks.

For the first belief given:
- a **simple** explanation of a relevant and accurate point (1 mark)
- a **detailed** explanation of a relevant and accurate point (2 marks)

For the second contrasting belief given:
- a **simple** explanation of a relevant and accurate point (1 mark)
- a **detailed** explanation of a relevant and accurate point (2 marks)

Answers might include:

Christians believe that God made all people free and equal. All were made in the image of God (Genesis 1:27). This entitles all to rights including that of freedom of religious expression. Dignitas Personae states that the 'human person has a right to religious freedom'. They point to the fact that Jesus invited people to follow him, and did not force them – allowing them to choose their religious path.

In Islam, it is acceptable to be a Christian or Jew – both are 'people of the book'. Converting to either from Islam is apostasy and carries the death penalty. The eastern religions are not accepted, and are seen as blasphemy, for example Hinduism as it worships deities.

Hints and tips

You have to give two **different** beliefs in the answer to this question – writing about one can only get you 2 out of 4 marks.

Always read the whole question including the instructions as this could be vital to prevent a wasted answer.

(d) Total of 4 marks + 1 mark

Look for explanation of two different teachings in the answer.

For the first teaching given:
- a **simple** explanation of a teaching which is both clearly relevant to the question and accurate (1 mark)
- a **detailed** explanation of a teaching which is both clearly relevant to the question and accurate (2 marks)

For the second teaching given:
- a **simple** explanation of a teaching which is both clearly relevant to the question and accurate (1 mark)
- a **detailed** explanation of a teaching which is both clearly relevant to the question and accurate (2 marks)

Relevant and accurate reference to scripture and/or sacred writing as required. (1 mark)

Answers might include:

Christianity – God created everyone equally, love your neighbour, the story of the Good Samaritan, we are all equal by being created in the image of God, 'there is neither Jew nor Gentile, slave or free man, male or female. We are all equal in Christ'.

Islam – Allah loves the fair minded, Muhammad allowed the Black African to make the call to prayer in Madinah, on hajj everyone is equal, and the Five Pillars apply to all, everyone is as equal as the teeth on a comb'.

Hints and tips

You have to explain two **different** teachings in the answer to this question.

The mark scheme tells you that the points have to be 'clearly relevant' – if you write something that does not make sense, or that you have to think about to make it relevant, then it is not a good answer.

A good way to answer is to give a teaching, and then explain how it is important.

You do not have to give exact quotations – it is fine to paraphrase. What you have to do is make it obvious that you are referring to something a person definitely said, and that what you say they said is approximately right. This is especially true when you are referring to a long teaching.

Using key technical terms is always very impressive to the examiner. Try to make sure you use them when you can.

(e) These questions are marked according to levels of response – this means your answer is judged for its quality overall, not for how many different arguments you present.

Answers might include:

Arguments in support of the view:

➤ *If we look at the causes there are far too many to deal with.*
➤ *Poverty is caused by problems like climate change, which humans have few answers for.*
➤ *Thousands die of starvation, disease and because of war every year.*
➤ *As the rich world gets richer the poor world gets poorer.*
➤ *New issues are happening – excessive loans, exploitation and people trafficking that are causing the problem to be worse.*
➤ *Poverty is now at such a level people are exploiting it to make money.*
➤ *Food and water are basic needs yet millions are without them.*
➤ *We have been trying to solve it for years yet the problem just seems to grow.*
➤ *From a religious perspective, as it contravenes all the teachings about helping the poor it is more a travesty than just a problem.*
➤ *Poverty contravenes so many religious teachings across all religions that it is the major concern for people in carrying out their religious duty.*

Arguments supporting other views:

➤ *There are many other issues as well – war, terrorism, finding cures for incurable diseases.*
➤ *For half the world, poverty does not affect them.*
➤ *Environmental issues which have the chance of destroying the planet are much more of a concern and actually a fundamental cause of poverty – so a greater problem.*
➤ *There are issues far greater than poverty, meaning that the religious ideas about stewardship and khalifah are not being met so religious people are failing God.*

Hints and tips

You need to make sure you give arguments to agree **and** to disagree with the statement – if you give only one point of view, then you cannot get above half marks.

Your answer must be full of religious content – this is a statement about religious beliefs and teachings.

The top level requires good development of the arguments you present. This means giving the argument and explaining clearly why it supports/contradicts the statement using detailed examples. This level is looking for a lot of development.

Try to get into the habit of offering three for and three against arguments in all your AO2 answers. Explain and provide examples for each, and include teachings if possible – this will help push your response to a higher level.